Three Minutes A Day

VOLUME 37

Other Christopher Books in Print

Better to Light One Candle
and other volumes in the
Three Minutes A Day
series

God Delights in You

World Religions

THREE MINUTES A DAY
VOLUME 37

The Christophers

Gerald Costello
President, The Christophers

Stephanie Raha
Editor-in-Chief

Margaret O'Connell
Senior Research Editor

Joan Bromfield
Edward J. Devane
Jonathan Englert
Monica Ann Yehle-Glick
Umberto Mignardi
Kimberley Mohabeer
Jerry O'Neil
Karen Hazel Radenbough
Anna Marie Tripodi
Anne Marie Welsh
Contributing Editors

The Christophers
12 East 48th Street
New York, NY 10017

This I call to mind, and therefore I have hope:

The steadfast love of the Lord never ceases,

His mercies never come to an end;

they are new every morning;

great is Your faithfulness.

"The Lord is my portion," says my soul,

"therefore I will hope in Him."

LAMENTATIONS 3:21-24

Introduction

The events of September 11, 2001 shook our world. After the shock and horror, people everywhere chose to answer with compassion and even holiness. Here's one such response.

This spring, several Christopher staff members staffed a booth at the annual National Catholic Educational Association convention where many delegates told us what a positive role our message has played in their lives.

One visitor's story stood out in a special way. She was a school administrator in upstate New York, who told us that after the terrorist attack on our nation her staff searched for a theme that would color their school's response – in assembly programs, letter to parents, conversations with individual students. It ultimately came from a Christopher prayer card with a simple but powerful Scriptural message: "Do not be overcome by evil, but overcome evil with good. (Romans 12:21)

"We found the right thing to say," our visitor said, "thanks to The Christophers."

After all these years, we're still doing our best to find the right thing to say. And, together, let's continue to illuminate the darkness with candles of faith, hope and, above all, love.

Jerry Costello
The Christophers

I've Looked at Clouds...

Sculptor and author Kent Nerburn once drove a cab for a living. One of his regular customers was a quiet, prim, blind woman. Over time, they became friends and eventually he asked her what she might like to see, if she could see for only a minute.

"Clouds," she said.

"As I drove along I pondered her words," recalls Nerburn. "I, who saw clearly, spent each day wishing for...a place, a person, some prize...I hoped to win. But one who valued sight the most, the one to whom it was denied, knew the greatest gift her eyesight could bestow was before me, unnoticed and unhallowed, at that very moment."

"Now let me ask you," the woman said. "What is a cloud like?"

"They're like God's dreams," he told her.

She thanked him, smiled, and they shared the rest of the ride in silence.

Open your mind, your senses, your soul to God's wonders.

O Lord...Your cloud stands over them and You go in front of them, in a pillar of cloud by day and in a pillar of fire by night. (Numbers 14:14)

Teach me to see You in everyday sights and hear You in everyday conversations.

Devotion to Sick Children

Actress Nancy Addison Altman has enjoyed a long and successful career in daytime television. She is also a volunteer. The former Emmy nominee spends part of her days at New York City's Incarnation Children's Center (ICC). There she befriended young HIV-positive patients. But it wasn't until she was diagnosed with cancer a few years ago that she found the "big parallel between me and those kids. We're fighting something, and we're determined to beat it."

Her cancer has spread, but Altman remains devoted to ICC and the youngsters it helps. She continues to organize fundraisers and solicit money, and the $3 million she has already raised has enabled the ICC to become a full-service facility for 120 outpatients. Despite the agonizing disease she herself endures, Altman insists, "If you're fortunate enough to have a good life, you have to give back."

Giving of oneself is its own reward.

The righteous are generous. (Psalm 37:21)

Remind us, Jesus, that if charity begins at home with ourselves and our nearest and dearest, so does generosity.

Acting Your Age?

You'd think that at 95, poet Stanley Kunitz might be slowing down.

Quite the contrary. Kunitz has grown more vigorous, fueled by his own intense lust for life and a rare gift for self-renewal. In fact, it was only at 95 that Kunitz received an honor bestowed upon only the most distinguished of American poets: Poet Laureate.

Although physically frail and a bit bent, his speech slightly slowed with age, Kunitz has indeed discovered an internal fountain of youth that keeps him going. "I don't wake up as a nonagenarian. I wake up each day as a poet," he says proudly.

At an age when many people have typically accepted that their best work is behind them, Kunitz is going full speed ahead.

What perceptions and images do you have of the elderly? How accurate are they?

How attractive is sound judgment...good counsel... wisdom...and understanding...in the venerable! (Sirach 25:4,5)

Jesus, the will to be productive and creative knows no age. Help us be considerate to those with more age and experience than we have.

Housekeeping 101

A friend with a keen sense of humor passed along some important rules of housekeeping. Enjoy them!

- Vacuuming too often weakens the carpet fibers.

- Rename the area under the couch the Galapagos Islands and claim an ecological exemption for the dust bunnies.

- Dirty film on windows and screens provide a filter against harmful and aging sunlight. You know, SPF 5, at least.

- Cobwebs reduce the glare from light bulbs and create a romantic mood.

- Genuinely out of control dusting? Put a showy urn on the coffee table and insist "THIS is where Grandma wanted us to scatter her ashes..."

Go ahead. Laugh! And remember, there is humor in many situations if you just look for it.

Sarah said, "God has brought laughter for me; everyone who hears will laugh with me." (Genesis 21:6)

Incarnate One, help us to find and enjoy the humorous in our daily lives.

Stories Speak to Us

Consider, for a moment, the ritual of the bedtime story. A child in pajamas snuggles up to listen to someone he or she loves very much recount a fascinating tale. In other words, it's about much more than the story itself.

So why does storytelling fall by the wayside as we get older? Novelist George Green recognizes its value, and has developed a series of wildly successful storytelling events.

"It seemed to me people were getting further and further apart," says Green. He had an innate understanding that good storytelling can create a sense of instant community.

"People like stories and they like gathering to hear stories," says Green.

Jesus knew this. He used parables to touch hearts. Those who gather in church each week continue to enjoy hearing His stories. They also benefit from the sense of community created.

The next time you hear the Bible being read, make an effort to really listen.

He began to teach them many things in parables. (Mark 4:2)

Draw us together, Lord God, through literature, the arts and our community.

Soothing Subways

What would it take to soothe your soul if you were a daily commuter on one of the world's crowded, pushy and otherwise unpleasant subways?

According to a newspaper columnist, many of the world's subway systems are crowded with riders but are too expensive to expand. So how can officials make things more pleasant while trains remain packed?

In Paris, with its 100-year-old system, officials used what the writer calls "a typically French fix–Let them have massages. And–bien sur!–food." In Stockholm, they hired "laughing instructors" to help riders feel better about being crushed into cars with too many others.

One New York rider said, "I want the back rubs, and…clowns." Others thought gift bags with little bottles of water and hand lotion, free magazines, even cookies would be good.

We may have different ideas of comfort, but even the simplest things mean a lot, so do what you can to comfort others.

This is my comfort in my distress, that Your promise gives me life. (Psalm 119:50)

Lord, may we find and share comfort in small things.

Making an Impact

The Jane Goodall Institute has this motto: "Every individual matters. Every individual has a role to play. Every individual makes a difference." The life of scientist and conservationist Dr. Goodall herself epitomizes it.

About 40 years ago, she established a field station in Tanzania and began her groundbreaking research into chimpanzees. Her work is so respected that she's been called "the Einstein of behavioral science."

Dr. Goodall believes that everyone shapes history. We can choose to have a positive or a negative impact on our world. She writes in her memoir, *Reason for Hope*, that we influence one another, "teacher and pupil, parent and child, world leader and citizen, writer or actor and the general public."

She adds, "Our knowledge of chimpanzee behavior does, indeed, indicate that our aggressive tendencies are deeply embedded in our primate heritage. Yet so too are our caring and altruistic ones."

What decisions will you make today?

Let us choose what is right. (Job 34:4)

Help us, Lord, to choose good and not evil.

Basket Task

Imagine passing the collection basket at church and being told to take $10 out. "It was a reverse offering," says Rev. Greg Barrette of Kansas City, who came up with the idea.

Barrette's church regularly gives ten percent of its monthly income to support a variety of needs. He resolved to let individual members, rather than the board, decide how the money should be spent one month.

"I thought, how neat that the board trusts us with the sacred honor of tithing and giving," says church member Nancy Fabiano.

She and her husband both gave their money to an organization buying back slaves in Africa. Others supported everything from the Special Olympics to hospitals.

Not surprisingly, friends and acquaintances increased the unique tithing effort significantly. Inspired by the plan, many donated their own money, too.

Use your ingenuity to support causes close to your heart.

Each of you must give as you have made up your mind, not reluctantly or under compulsion, for God loves a cheerful giver. (2 Corinthians 9:7)

Let us not fear sharing Your resources, God.

Watch the Cholesterol

We need to be smarter about our hearts, warns Dr. Scott Grundy, chairman of the National Cholesterol Education Program. "Americans are not in good shape. They eat too many saturated fats and they're overweight," says the doctor.

Because heart disease is linked to high cholesterol levels, Dr. Grundy and his colleagues recommend tripling the number of adults who should be taking cholesterol-lowering drugs.

And 65 million adults should be on a cholesterol-lowering diet. Dr. Grundy insists the aggressive plan is necessary, and that the cholesterol guidelines should be considered a "wake-up call" for Americans.

Help yourself today. Make an appointment for a physical and start an exercise program. Enjoy lots of fruits and vegetables, eat less red meat and fatty foods and avoid deep fried food.

You only have one heart and one life. Do what you can to stay healthy.

It was You who formed my inward parts; You knit me together in my mother's womb. (Psalm 139:13)

May I value the gift of life today and every day, Spirit of God.

Failure to Understand

"We're taught to be afraid of failure," says Terry Gross, award-winning radio host of National Public Radio's *Fresh Air*. "Sometimes when you fail, it's for a good reason."

Such was the case in her life. While in college, she abandoned her dreams of becoming a writer, deciding her efforts didn't measure up. Instead, she headed for a junior high classroom in Buffalo. "I was a disaster as a teacher," she says simply. After six weeks on the job, she was fired.

"I was glad they fired me," says Gross. She believes people often remain in bad situations and lack the courage to leave because they don't want to be seen as quitters.

"Sometimes, as in my case," she observes, "the failure is doing you a favor."

However good or bad the circumstances, learn from them.

Take courage, all you people...says the Lord; work, for I am with you. (Haggai 2:4)

Give me wisdom, Holy One, to embrace failure and move on.

Talking to Your Children

Of course, you talk to your children. But are they listening? And do you listen to them?

Susan Alexander Yates, author of *And Then I Had Teenagers,* offers tips to help parents improve communication with their children.

1. When they're little, do something with them daily. For older children, be available for conversation.

2. Asking, "Tell me something interesting you learned today" requires more than a one-word answer.

3. Teach respect. For instance, show them how to disagree without being verbally abusive.

4. Pay attention to their conversation. Make their friends welcome in your home.

5. Communicate with your son or daughter based on their interests and gifts.

6. Be encouraging. Stay positive and supportive. Building a happy home takes daily work.

Honor your father, and do not forget the birth pangs of your mother. (Sirach 7:27)

May we always keep open the lines of communication, God, between ourselves and our children.

Perpetually Dissatisfied?

In spite of many problems, America is in its Golden Age according to Gregg Easterbrook, an editor at *The New Republic*. Yet, in his opinion, everybody keeps complaining.

"By almost every measure," Easterbrook said, "life in the United States today is the best it has ever been...." But he then goes on to cite poll data showing that the percentage of Americans describing themselves as happy hasn't increased since the 1950s.

What's going on? Maybe the polls are wrong or incomplete; or the data is being misinterpreted; or people are dissatisfied because they are always striving so hard, no achievement is ever really enough.

Whether or not you think these are the best of times–or the worst of times–complaining by itself accomplishes nothing. Ask yourself what constructive action you can take to solve dilemmas. And above all, count your blessings.

Offer to God a sacrifice of thanksgiving. (Psalm 50:14)

Remind me, God, that I have a universe to appreciate–and most of all, I have You.

A Second Wind

In increasing numbers, people in their 40s, 50s and 60s are taking up new careers. Dr. Roy Yeager, a Manhattan dentist sold his practice after 33 years. Now he is a psychotherapist.

As Yeager sees it, when people approach middle age they can either drift or they can decide "to act—to do something different." What he most enjoyed about being a dentist was listening to his patients and getting to know them. His second career provides a chance to pursue this interest.

Yeager earned degrees in social work and psychotherapy, and set up what is now a growing practice. Dr. Yeager, who has no intention of fading into old age, is proof that life isn't over just because you are getting older.

You are never too old to change, to renew your life.

If riches are a desirable possession...what is richer than wisdom? (Wisdom of Solomon 8:5)

Christ my Lord, inspire me to gladly grasp all change that is for the better.

A Web Site for Every Hobby

At one time, it seemed everyone had a hobby. From coin collecting to paper dolls, hobbies were encouraged and cultivated. Then, the majority of us appeared to follow more passive pursuits, or simply worked longer hours at our jobs. Today, thanks to the Internet, the hobbyist has been rejuvenated.

Stamps, coins, jewelry, and even barbed wire–you name the pastime and there is surely a Web site for and about it. Instant communication about the tiniest specialties is possible on the Net, along with an increased audience for each. One in four online visitors check out hobby and lifestyle sites for a total of 8 million hours in one month. *About.com* has 45 hobby sites. Its most popular include quilting, cross-stitching, bird watching, radio-controlled vehicles and genealogy.

Hobbies are a labor of love born of passion. Pick a hobby and let it rekindle your natural-born curiosity. It will keep you young at heart.

Go, eat your bread with enjoyment, and drink your wine with a merry heart. (Ecclesiastes 9:7)

May I appreciate and cherish the child in me, Abba.

For Ancestors and Children

Money can be very important. But for the Gullah-speaking people of South Carolina's Sea Islands, it could threaten their culture.

These descendants of African slaves have retained their language and African customs through their ties to the land. Now, in the face of distant relatives keen on selling to developers, the local Gullah people are making their stand.

They have formed a coalition to close zoning loopholes and established laws prohibiting gated communities, golf courses and resorts. According to Marquetta Goodwine, founder of the Gullah/Geechee Sea Island Coalition, "Gullah can survive...only if the people can hold onto their land and teach their children about their traditions."

Many of us let traditions go because of time or financial constraints or lack of interest. Yet how can we and our children face the future without remembering the past? For tomorrow's sake, let's respect our heritage and our neighbors?

Let us now sing the praises of...our ancestors. (Sirach 44:1)

Guide us, God, that we may teach our children to honor their heritage and others.

Teaching Kindness to Kids

The five words on the poster were simple and eloquent: KINDNESS IS CONTAGIOUS... CATCH IT! When Barbara Unell read them, she knew she had found an answer to the problem of teaching children to be kind to each other.

"All children have the capacity to be both cruel and kind," says Unell, the mother of two children, author of parenting books, and director of a family education center in Kansas City, Missouri. "When I saw those words...I knew there was a way for schools to teach children how to do the right thing."

Ten years after its founding, her *Kindness Is Contagious* program is used in more than 400 schools in the Kansas City area. Unell believes that teaching kindness is as important as teaching math and reading, and recommends that kindness start at home.

Spread some kindness around you today. It's contagious!

Show kindness and mercy to one another; do not oppress the widow, the orphan, the alien, or the poor. (Zechariah 7:9-10)

Lord, how many need our kindnesses! Help us.

Never Too Late for Apologies

Nearly six decades after he almost died at the hands of a frenzied mob in war-torn Germany, 76-year-old Sidney Brown returned to the industrial town of Ruesselsheim to receive an apology from its citizens.

In 1944, a teenaged Brown and seven fellow airmen were shot down and captured. Passing through Ruesselsheim two days later, they were attacked by a group of townspeople seeking revenge after a night of allied bombing raids. Only Brown and one other man were spared and later spent the rest of the war as prisoners.

Brown thought long and hard before going back to the town. Yet, even before the moving memorial ceremony he eventually attended, Brown said he had long since forgiven the people of the town. "I have no animosity in my heart against the people of Germany or the people of Ruesselsheim."

No matter what the circumstances, both seeking and granting forgiveness is good for our hearts and souls.

Forgive us our sins for we ourselves forgive everyone indebted to us. (Luke 11:4)

May we let go of angry and negative emotions, Merciful Savior.

The Challenge of Leadership

What is the meaning of the word LEADERSHIP?

Here's one interpretation from a periodical of the same name:

L Love what you do. Let others know it.

E Express yourself tactfully.

A Ask questions and keep on learning.

D Do the right thing.

E Enthusiasm is contagious. Spread it around!

R Respond to all inquiries.

S Share your knowledge.

H Hope for the best; don't be pessimistic.

I Intuition is powerful; heed your gut feeling.

P Patience is a virtue, one appreciated by all.

Take on the challenge of leadership in your business, personal and family life. Practice it daily and diligently.

A people's leader is proved wise by his words. (Sirach 9:17)

My Lord, lead me in seeking Your will, in doing the right thing.

Many Causes, One World

Biologist and activist Nell Newman spent several years soliciting money to save endangered birds of prey. However, it was difficult to maintain interest among her donors once the birds were down-listed from endangered to threatened.

Turning to her father, actor and philanthropist Paul Newman, she discovered a way to fund the organizations directly. The result? Newman's Own Organics, an organic food company that donates 100 per cent of its after-tax profits to charities ranging from reestablishing endangered species to protecting rainforests to building adequate housing for those in impoverished areas.

Nell Newman, with her father's guidance, has taken a cause dear to her heart and transformed it into an altruistic empire bent on helping the world one mission at a time.

Each and every one of us can do our part to promote our own special cause, to better our corner of the world.

Do good. (1 Peter 3:11)

Your world is marvelous, Heavenly Father. Grant us the compassion and fortitude to protect it.

A Thousand Points of Light or Just One?

At some time or another, you may have noticed a particularly brilliant night sky, replete with twinkling stars. If you thought each of those twinkling points of light were individual stars, think again.

Contrary to appearances, the majority of stars are not individuals, but rather systems of multiple stars so far away that they appear to be a single entity to us on Earth.

This discovery was the work of British astronomer William Herschel, who, in the late eighteenth century, began the first comprehensive telescopic survey of the stars. He found "doubles" everywhere and soon realized that many of these consisted of two stars vastly distant from each other, but coincidentally lying along a single line of sight, a visual phenomena called optical doubles.

With people as with stars, it's always a good idea to look closely before making judgments. And when we are wrong, to ask forgiveness.

If there is repentance, you must forgive. (Luke 17:3)

Lord God, give me Your good counsel to judge carefully—and to ask forgiveness.

Book Author, Book Lover, Book Seller

Not many people would try to take on Amazon, the mammoth Internet bookseller. But Larry McMurtry, the Pulitzer Prize winning author of such books as *Lonesome Dove, Terms of Endearment* and *The Last Picture Show,* is doing just that.

McMurtry watched with dismay as bookstore after bookstore closed unable to compete with books sold on the Internet and rising real estate prices. The author started Booked Up, a giant used bookstore of his own in his hometown of Archer City, Texas. He dreams of turning sleepy Archer City, population 1,748, into "book town," a place for serious bibliophiles to browse and shop.

Although only one bookseller has decided to move to Archer City so far, McMurtry believes the low rents and spacious stores will make it happen. In the meantime, things aren't so bad: Booked Up is making a profit.

If something's important to you, maybe it's important to others, too. Ask yourself what practical ways you can do good.

Keep alert, stand firm in your faith, be courageous, be strong. Let all that you do be done in love. (1 Corinthians 16:13-14)

Give us Your courage, Lord God, to use the talents You have given us.

Reading Churches

"Churches are narratives," says Margaret Visser, "stories that use...symbols and design practices to enlighten, educate, and induce emotion in the people who enter them."

In *The Geometry of Love: Space, Time, Mystery, and Meaning in an Ordinary Church,* Visser, using the church of St. Agnes Outside the Walls in Rome, offers detailed explanations of the seemingly ordinary things that make up the church building, as well as the words, clothing and customs associated with churches.

In her walk through, around and under this Italian church, Visser enlightens readers curious about architecture, Christianity, and the varied aspects connected with places of worship–"often the oldest, and usually the most famous, the strangest, the most beautiful buildings any town has to offer."

Pay attention to the story of the next church you visit. Look and listen with mind and heart.

Aquila and Prisca, together with the church in their house, greet you warmly in the Lord. (1 Corinthians 16:19)

I offer You praise, Lord, in the silence of a church, in...the church within me, in the church which is my family.

The Tradition of the Trail

As Jerry Martinez takes a moment of rest during his 150-mile horseback ride from Eagle Pass, Texas, to San Antonio, he observes his companions and the pale, dry Texas brush country.

"I guess it's kind of desolate out here, but that's the way we like it," he says.

He is one of nearly 5,000 people who make their way each year on horseback to the "Alamo City," as part of a 47-year-old tradition of trail riding. They typically travel only 20 to 25 miles a day. Jerry Martinez, a private detective from Abilene, adds, "We generally take it kind of slow and easy, and that makes the ride a lot of fun and a good way to know the people you're traveling with."

The journey ends when the riders converge at the annual San Antonio Stock Show and Rodeo.

Traditional activities keep elements of our culture and history alive. What helps you keep in touch with your heritage?

The boundary lines have fallen for me in pleasant places; I have a goodly heritage. (Psalm 16:6)

God, remind me to think of the past as well as of the future as I go about my life.

Finding Healing in Dreams

At the foot of the Turkish hill on which sprawl the ruins of the once mighty city of Pergamum lie remains of the Asclepieum, a spa long popular with ancient Greeks and Romans.

In its heyday, the Asclepieum was famed for its holy spring and for its physician-priests, who encouraged their patients to eat wisely, to exercise frequently—and to dream. Patients spent the night in the temple. A priest would wander among them, dressed as Asclepius, the Greek god of healing, accompanied by sacred snakes, dogs or geese. The main goal was to help patients have a night of god-inspired dreams which might produce cures.

If the dreams of the night didn't produce cures, they were discussed, interpreted and followed as a prescription.

What the ancients knew, modern science confirms: people are a union of mind and body. What troubles one, troubles the other; what heals one, heals the other. Heed both for optimal health.

Happy are those who find wisdom.
(Proverbs 3:13)

Today, Creator, I offer all I do in thanks-giving for the gifts You have given me.

Set the Stage for Business

If "all the world's a stage," even business might take a cue from Shakespeare. At least that's the opinion of Sean Kavanagh of the Ariel Group, a Boston-based, executive training program.

Kavanagh feels that much of Shakespeare is about leadership and the truth that one leadership style is not enough. "Depending on the situation," Kavanagh says, "the business chief may need to be a tyrant, a captain or democratic."

Program participants are invited to act out a scene and to envision that scene in the workplace. For example, a CEO can learn to deal with *Romeo and Juliet's* Tybalt-type character, the young, hotheaded member of the company who battles the boss.

The best students, according to Kavanagh, are the senior executives who "are more comfortable with who they are, are much more willing to read Shakespeare with extreme gusto. They encourage the younger folks."

Live "with extreme gusto." Encourage those around you to do the same.

Learn a lesson. (Jeremiah 35:13)

Lead me, Master, help me to find You and celebrate Your gifts to me this day.

A Gift for Life

In a courageous act of generosity, one family who'd suffered the death of their eight-year-old boy brought life and joy to another.

Doctors had told Luke Harbur's parents that their infant probably wouldn't live to see his second birthday because of a liver disease known as Alagille syndrome. "We knew that without a liver transplant Luke would die," said his mother, Kim. And no donor livers were available.

But when eight-year-old Aaron Drake lay dying his mother contacted the Harburs and donated his liver, which was compatible.

In Aaron's honor, the Harburs founded Gift of Life Foundation to raise awareness of the importance of organ donation.

Said Mrs. Harbur, "Our son is now a happy, healthy five-year-old because of one family's willingness to give us that gift."

Are you willing to seriously consider making such a gift yourself?

The measure you give will be the measure you get, and still more will be given you. (Mark 4:24)

Creator, how can I celebrate and share the gift of life with Your children in need?

Special Dogs with Special Jobs

Ike picks things up, turns light switches on and off, loads the clothes dryer and takes dishes from the dishwasher. He'll even sort recyclables and bring the telephone closer. Ike, a yellow Labrador with special training, is Elizabeth Twohy's teammate.

As the director of disability services for Brookdale Community College in New Jersey, she doesn't see herself as Ike's master. Rather, she believes that his presence allows her to keep working.

Similar in some ways to guide dogs for blind people, "service dogs" make life easier for those with physical disabilities. "People see somebody in a wheelchair and shy away," said Laura Dubecky, instructor at the Canine Companions for Independence Center. "Add a dog to that picture (and) people will come right up and talk...It can be a help to self-esteem."

Do you judge people by their appearance and abilities? Or do you look beneath the surface?

You judge by human standards; I judge no one. (John 8:15)

Merciful Savior, whenever we judge others or ourselves by human standards, show us how to imitate Your mercifulness instead.

Welcome to the Community Office Space

The "open" floor plan office is, most likely, here to stay. Supporters say it improves communication and promotes teamwork. Critics say it affords employees neither privacy nor quiet time to get work done.

How can you create a sense of privacy when there are no walls between you and your co-workers?

- Ask management for an "escape room," where employees can have private conversations or brainstorming sessions.
- Leave your office to use a cell or pay phone for personal conversations.
- Create "walls" with plants, bookcases and framed pictures.
- Deflect interruptions with body language: eyes down or fixed on your computer screen, body turned into your space.

We all need quiet periods throughout the day for work, reflection and prayer. Find ways to get even three minutes a day of solitude and quiet. It will restore your spirit!

Since we are justified by faith, we have peace with God through our Lord Jesus Christ. (Romans 5:1)

Jesus, send us Your Holy Spirit to comfort us.

Grasping Homelessness, Firsthand

It was volunteer Robin Schoettler Fox's turn to spend a night at her community's shelter for homeless families. She selected the unmade mattress in the center of the room for herself.

But before sleep, she helped clean the kitchen and put out sandwiches for the next day's bag lunches. Then the volunteer spent time with Nicole, a junior-high student who had to take a quiz to improve a grade from B+ to an A. Nicole said to Fox, "We're still people, we're just homeless."

The next morning, the volunteer took a hard look at the folks around her: "Their faces? They look a lot like mine."

Volunteering can help point out the similarities, as well as the differences, between those who have and those who don't. Tend to the needs of others and you will bridge that gap.

Let each of you look not to your own interests, but to the interests of others. Let the same mind be in you that was in Christ Jesus. (Philippians 2:4-5)

What can each one of us do to care for homeless people, Redeemer?

Rules of the Game of Life

Hilary Oliver coaches girls from elementary through high school for gymnastic competitions and for life.

The coordinator and head coach of the Davis, California, gymnastics team promotes healthy attitudes about body image by cautioning her fellow coaches not to complain about their figures. The girls are told, "your body needs fuel; you're asking it to do amazing things," she says.

While helping her team master the balance beam, Oliver also helps them balance competitiveness with caring, and promotes healthy attitudes about life. At each weekly team meeting, the girls are encouraged to compliment each other.

Says Susan Klasing, who has two girls in Oliver's program, "It's really about making better kids, using gymnastics to teach about life and life skills. She's big on things like manners, respect, being kind to one another."

Show respect and kindness to others and to yourself. Life will be better.

Render true judgments, show kindness and mercy to one another. (Zechariah 7:9)

Make me an instrument of Your justice and love, Father.

Doing For Others

"And what did you do for someone today?" That was the question Doctor Jack McConnell's father used to ask each of his seven children over dinner. Years later, Dr. McConnell is doing quite a bit for those less fortunate than he is.

After moving to a gated retirement community in Hilton Head, South Carolina, the doctor discovered that many of the locals who make the island community function had little or no access to medical care.

Dr. McConnell set out to do something about it. It took a few years to set up, but today a thriving clinic called *Volunteers in Medicine* attends to the needs of thousands of patients. Staffed by retired physicians, nurses and dentists, the free clinic's success has spawned a number of VIM facilities all over the country.

Dr. McConnell's father left him a valuable legacy. Ask yourself the question: What did I do for someone today?

A man was going down from Jerusalem to Jericho...A Samaritan...was moved with pity. (Luke 10:29,33)

Jesus, inspire me to do for others as though for You.

Window on the Past

On Sunday mornings at Chicago's New Mount Pilgrim Missionary Baptist Church, a stained-glass window looms behind the Rev. Marshall Hatch as he preaches. At its center is the Christ-like figure of a muscular black man. His body forms the pit of a slave ship.

The window symbolizes the route millions of Africans traveled to the Americas. Called "Maafu Remembrance," a Swahili word which means unspeakable horror, it refers to the horrors of the Middle Passage, the slave trade.

Rev. Hatch and others hope that depictions of their enslaved ancestors can help worshippers connect to God. As he says, "It makes me whole to remember that this is what I've come through to get where I am. This passes down to our children."

Remembering the past is agonizing for many who have suffered, but it is necessary if we are to embrace the present and create a better future.

Our God has not forsaken us in our slavery, but has extended to us His steadfast love. (Ezra 9:9)

Lord our deliverer, help us to make something positive out of painful experiences.

Prayer and Modern Medicine

When it comes to healing illnesses of the body and mind, holistic methods are growing in popularity. However, whether religion and spirituality can actually heal what ails us is a controversial issue within the scientific community.

Medical literature worldwide has recorded more than 1200 recent studies on the health and religion-spirituality relationship. Researchers are reporting constantly on the positive effects of prayer on patients with cancer, AIDS and heart disease. As reported in a prestigious medical journal, researchers found documented differences in recovery rates between cardiac patients who were prayed for by volunteer strangers and those who were not. The prayed-for patients, according to the study, did 11 percent better.

And more medical schools across North America are offering conferences and courses in spirituality.

Prayer, spirituality and a positive mind-set are powerful in a way we may never fully understand, but which can contribute to our well-being.

The Lord is good to those who wait for Him, to the soul that seeks Him. (Lamentations 3:25)

Holy Spirit, I ask for Your healing intercession.

Good Coffee and Better Friends

Gathering to talk about life in an informal and fun way can be good medicine. Jane Heitman and five friends started a coffee klatch that has grown into an important part of each of their lives.

At these get-togethers, Heitman says, "we've loved and supported each other through work problems, the deaths of parents and personal injuries. Sometimes we trade recipes, books and shopping tips."

This diverse group of a retail clerk, two clerical workers and three teachers, has found that listening to each other's stories with sympathy and understanding has helped them weather many storms.

It doesn't matter if they share the same problems, whether they are married or not, have children or don't. What matters is that they can share sadness and celebrate the joys in each other's lives.

Enjoy the pleasures of friendship as often as you can.

Do not abandon old friends, for new ones cannot equal them. A new friend is like new wine; when it has aged, you can drink it with pleasure. (Sirach 9:10)

Jesus, bless us with good friends. And bless our friendships.

Information Overload

When Adam Gardner accessed the Internet to research the historic Hindenberg blimp explosion for his eight-year-old nephew, he expected to find articles related only to that aviation tragedy. He didn't expect to be connected to a link about building one's own "Hindenberg Bomb" at home.

Alarmed—and hoping his nephew hadn't also been connected to such information—Gardner called his Internet provider to ask how such information could be so easily accessible. He was especially concerned because he had ordered his Internet service with child-protection restrictions that ought to have blocked dangerous material. The unsatisfactory answer was that they tried to block obscenity, but did not have the technology to block all dangerous information.

We are truly each other's keeper. Vigilance is one way of protecting people, especially children, from harm. That's one of the greatest kindnesses we can do.

A person is justified by works and not by faith alone. ...As the body without the spirit is dead, so faith without works is also dead.
(James 2:24,26)

Guide me, Jesus, to Your chosen path for me.

Investing in Friendship

When a group of wealthy partners purchased a rare multimillion-dollar violin, they were investing to support a musician friend, not to make an immediate economic return.

"That really isn't what it's about for me," said John Townsend. "It's about my friendship with Bobby. The more I learned about the importance of this instrument to how he defines himself as an artist, the more I realized that we had to find a way to make this happen."

The partners were helping Robert McDuffie, a respected violinist who hoped to take his career to another level. He described the rare violin as "more than an extension of my body. It was an extension of my musical personality."

McDuffie's part of the arrangement is to play the instrument so it maintains its value.

It seems everything comes out a winner: the arts, the artist, audiences, and the ongoing value of friendship.

Is friendship vital to your life?

When you gain friends, gain them through testing. (Sirach 6:7)

Bless our friends and acquaintances, Lord of life.

Reading to Youngsters

A survey for a *USA Today* study of parents reveals a sad truth: they aren't reading to children enough:

- 28 percent never read to them.
- Another 17 percent answered "Rarely."
- 3 percent weren't sure how often they read to their children.

In a world that includes the temptations of drugs and sex, as well as the threat of violence, at least 48 percent of parents are missing an important opportunity to spend time with children. It isn't all bad news though:

- 9 percent of the respondents indicated that they read to their children at least once a week.
- 15 percent do it several times weekly.
- 20 percent do it daily!

There's no way to shield children from the world which they will one day run, but you can make strong bonds and share healthy information to prepare them for a life of rewarding choices.

Train children in the right way. (Proverbs 22:6)

Father, may we raise children to know Your love.

When Life Is for the Birds

For the past ten years, Frank Viola, 82, one of several hundred pigeon racers in New York City, has invited fellow breeders—some from as far as Texas and Hawaii—to enter the "Frank Viola Invitational."

Like other pigeon racers, he takes great joy in watching the heavens for a homer returning to its loft. "If I wasn't flying pigeons, I'd be dead," he says. "My birds are my life."

Pigeon racing can be traced back to the Roman Empire. Unlike a horse race, a pigeon race involves an invisible course. Birds are trucked to a spot some 500 miles away and then freed as a flock to head back to their owners who wait, not cheering on the sidelines, but anxiously at their coops.

What's your favorite hobby or recreation? If you don't have one, get one. It will enrich your life.

When a bird flies...(the) air, lashed by the beat of its pinions and pierced by...its rushing flight, is traversed by the movement of its wings. (Wisdom of Solomon 5:11)

My heart rests in You, Lord. May I find peace and joy.

Family Commitments

Having a strong, happy family takes work and a commitment to the good of each individual, as well as the whole family.

- Family members must at times forgo their own immediate gratification to benefit another.

- All people like to be appreciated, including members of your family. Try "I really like the way that you…"

- Spend time together even if you're "too busy."

- Healthy humor is a family healer and unifier.

- Praying together can be a profound bonding experience.

- Tell each other about your day. Make each family member important to everyone else.

- Develop a language of acceptance: "words that value feelings, responses that change moods, answers that call for goodwill, and replies that radiate respect," says child psychologist Haim Ginott.

**Honor your father and your mother.
(Matthew 15:4)**

Bless every family, Creator.

Words for the Wise

If you want to expand your vocabulary, Anu Garg, a computer scientist from India, can help. In 1994, Garg, then a scholarship student nearing the end of his master's studies, started what has since become one of the most successful services on the Internet: AWAD (A Word A Day).

Each day, AWAD, which can be found at www.wordsmith.org, offers a different word along with its definition, etymology and a quote showing its use and maybe even a few reflections about it. Garg typically picks obscure words like Lazaretto (a hospital treating contagious diseases) or Podsnap (a person embodying insular complacency and self-satisfaction).

For Garg, whose site is visited by tens of thousands of people every day, English with its enormous vocabulary of two million words is virtually inexhaustible. "English never met a word it didn't like," mused Garg, a true logomaniac.

Celebrate language. Speak it well. Use it for good.

Remember the word that I said to you, "Servants are not greater than their master." (John 15:20)

Teach us Your language of loving fidelity, Jesus.

Choosing Integrity

Decisions. Decisions. Ethical decisions.

Compare the "rightness" of your decisions with this checklist based on Harry Emerson Fosdick's "Six-Point Test":

- Based on the facts, does what you've decided to do seem logical and reasonable?
- If another person decided to do the same thing, would you still think the action right?
- How do you think others will view your decision?
- What would the person you most admire do in this situation?
- Will you still think you did the right thing in ten years?
- How would you feel, and, what would your friends and family think, if your decision aired on a local TV or radio news program?

How do your decisions measure up? Are you proud of yourself? Is God proud of you?

Teach us...that we may gain a wise heart. (Psalm 90:12)

Give us, Jesus, the courageous wisdom to decide rightly.

A Good Man

Charles Schulz earned his lowest school grade in drawing. But that didn't stop him from pursuing a career as a cartoonist.

In 1948, he sold a single-panel comic, "L'il Folks," to the *St. Paul Pioneer Press*. When the paper refused to run it more than once a week, he offered it to United Feature Syndicate, which changed the name to "Peanuts."

For more than a half-century, millions delighted in the antics of Charlie Brown, Linus, Lucy, Schroeder, and so many others–not forgetting Snoopy, of course–learning lessons about faith, hope and love. When he put down his pen in January, 2000–he drew every single strip himself–he was facing Parkinson's disease and colon cancer. He died just a month later.

In the charming, thoughtful words and images he drew, we still get a glimpse of the good man who was Charles Schulz.

Do you let others see your goodness?

Let your light shine before others, so that they may see your good works and give glory to your Father in heaven. (Matthew 5:16)

In times of joy and in times of sorrow, You are with us, Father, celebrating and comforting.

Long Struggle for Justice

When he was 10 years old, the late Rev. Leon H. Sullivan conducted a one-man campaign against segregation at his local West Virginia drugstore after being told he couldn't drink his soda at the counter.

Throughout his life the clergyman and civil rights leader continued to fight for justice in this country and in South Africa.

He was responsible for "The Sullivan Principles," that urged businesses to treat their workers in South Africa in the same fair and nondiscriminatory manner as those in the U.S. Rev. Sullivan, a member of the board of General Motors, was able to persuade virtually all American companies to abide by the Sullivan Principles. When apartheid continued, he called for the companies to leave South Africa and the U.S. to impose sanctions. In time, apartheid was overthrown.

The long struggle points to the need for perseverance while struggling for all worthwhile social change.

Run with perseverance the race that is set before us. (Hebrews 12:1)

Give us Your gift of perseverance, Father-Creator.

You Must Remember This

When you are tempted to forget that you are unique and one of a kind, remember that you are special – and that a little of your loving kindness goes a long way for those around you.

Did a friend take extra time to really listen to you recently? Select a beautiful card and send a note, thanking him or her for your friendship.

Is your spouse overworked? Take his or her car on your errands next weekend. While you're out, fill up the gas tank, drive it through the car wash, vacuum it, and tuck a candy bar in the glove compartment.

Do you have an elderly relative nearby? Call to see if he or she needs anything like soap, stamps, or pens. Then drop by for a visit with your care package. Ask this person to share remembrances of growing up. What was his or her favorite way to spend a summer day as a child?

Do ordinary things in an extraordinary way.

Bear fruit in every good work. (Colossians 1:10)

Show us, Lord, how we can challenge ourselves to be extraordinary.

Busy with Life and Love

"The news of my passing is a bit premature," said 83-year-old Madeleine L'Engle, author of more than 50 books and writer-in-residence and librarian at Manhattan's Cathedral Church of St. John the Divine.

Although she hasn't gotten around much in the last few years because of a broken hip, L'Engle assures her readers that she is alive and still writing: "I'm busier than ever, and I'm feeling quite well."

Her most famous and enduring work, *A Wrinkle in Time,* about a girl who has to rescue her father from evil forces, is one of the best-selling children's books of all time.

About her only complaint: she misses her late husband of 40 years, actor Hugh Franklin. "In life I'm fine," she says. "But I wish I was in love."

We all need to share love–and to live life as fully as possibly, no matter what our age.

How attractive is sound judgment in the gray-haired, and for the aged to possess good counsel! How attractive is wisdom...and understanding and counsel in the venerable! (Sirach 25:4-5)

Lord, help me to live and love each moment of my life.

Then and Now

While it's difficult to scientifically measure emotions such as happiness and anxiety, Case Western Reserve University has completed a study which seems to indicate that children are considerably more anxious today than kids were in the 1950s.

If you are concerned about the young people in your life, Christine Gorman, writing in *Time* magazine, provides ideas that may help them cope. "Strengthening social ties protects against stress," she says. To this end, make a greater effort to connect one-on-one with your children, limit television and computer games, and plan activities your family can enjoy together.

"Keep your expectations for your children reasonable," says Gorman. For example, an ivy-league education is not a prerequisite to success.

Consistent and sufficient sleep and exercise are recommended, since levels of both are known to affect moods.

These are good reminders for both young people and the adults who love them.

I will both lie down and sleep in peace; for You alone, O Lord, make me lie down in safety. (Psalm 4:8)

Help me Spirit of Love, reach out to those around me in need.

Knitting Together

"It's a classic labor of love," says actress Tyne Daly. "There's something personal in every stitch," Daly says referring to her hobby of more than 40 years, knitting.

She compares knitting to yoga. "There's a rhythm to knitting that can settle the spirit and quiet you down," she says.

Daly and other actors on the TV series *Judging Amy*, who have caught her knitting bug, have found a way to make their knitting time even more productive. Together, they have created more than 130 baby caps, which they either give away to loved ones or sell. Proceeds from the sale of the caps go to an organization in Santa Monica that helps people living with cancer.

We have so many opportunities to do some good for other people. We just need to take advantage of the time and talents with which God has blessed us.

Provoke one another to love and good deeds. (Hebrews 10:24)

Thank you, God, for new ideas and creative ways to express Your love.

A Young George Washington

There's much that's common knowledge about George Washington. But there are lesser-known facts as well.

Yes, Washington and the Continental Army crossed the Delaware River. But a voyage he made as a 19-year-old isn't as known though it had implications for his career as Commander in Chief of the Continental Army.

In 1751 the future president accompanied his ailing half-brother, Lawrence, to Barbados. The hope was that a Caribbean visit would cure Lawrence's tuberculosis. It didn't. He died the following year.

Meanwhile, George Washington caught small-pox. And with it he acquired life-long immunity to the infectious disease. Later, when the Continental Army was devastated by the disease, General Washington remained healthy.

There are always new things to learn about even major historical figures of whom much has been written. The same is true for each one of us. Let's respect the individuality of all.

Why do you see the speck in your neighbor's eye, but do not notice the log in your own eye? (Luke 6:41)

May we remember we are more than meets the eye, Redeemer.

A "Delicious Revolution"

When New Jersey native Alice Waters opened her Berkeley, California restaurant, Chez Panisse, 30 years ago, she had no idea she'd later be credited with starting a revolution.

"I just knew I wanted to change the way my little community was eating," she said. Her interest in healthy, fresh food had been strengthened as a college student in France.

"When you buy fast food, you get fast-food values....labor is cheap, food is cheap, people should eat in a hurry, children should be entertained while they're eating, everything should be the same all the time."

At Chez Panisse, Waters introduced the use of fresh organically grown produce, in season, from local farmers. "This is the way people have eaten since the beginning of time," she observes. She extols farmers' markets as great places to appreciate the change of seasons. "And there's always something inexpensive because it's so plentiful."

Treasure the bounty God has given for our welfare.

Do not hate hard labor or farm work, which was created by the Most High. (Sirach 7:15)

Help us, God, to appreciate Your good earth.

Staying Youthful

Is it possible to be mentally young regardless of one's chronological age? According to author Deepak Chopra you can "grow younger and live longer" by cultivating a mind which is "dynamic, vibrant and curious...enthusiastic, spontaneous, fluid and adaptable."

Chopra suggests that these traits will help:

Enthusiasm–Greek for "filled with the divine"

Spontaneity–alert to new possibilities

Fluidity and Adaptability–life is interrelated

Playfulness and Lightheartedness–helps the immune system

Sensory Awareness–see everything with fresh eyes

Imagination

Learning and Growing

Whatever your age, enjoy every moment.

The days of our life are seventy years, or perhaps eighty, if we are strong. (Psalm 90:10)

From discrimination against older people, deliver us, Good Lord.

A Hospice for Children

Sister Frances Dominica, an Anglican nun, was discouraged from opening a hospice for youngsters with life-threatening illnesses but, convinced of the need for such a facility, went ahead.

So began England's Helen House in 1982, the world's first children's hospice. Now there is a network of them. Everyone, regardless of religious beliefs, is welcome at Helen House. The hospice also caters to the siblings of sick children with residential weekends and trips. Where necessary, it provides "dignified, terminal care."

Families who have lost a child are offered bereavement counseling for as long as they want it or need it.

"We see ourselves as advocates for the families," said Sister Frances Dominica. "We will not let them down."

If you have an idea you are convinced is good, don't be discouraged. Carry it out. You never know who might be helped.

Whoever welcomes one such child in My Name welcomes Me. (Matthew 18:5)

Grant us the strength to persevere in trying times, Merciful Savior.

Musical Medicine

Need a mood lift? How about something to calm your nerves? The answer may lie in your radio or compact disc player.

"The music we listen to affects how we feel, think and act," says Elizabeth Miles, the author of *Tune Your Brain: Using Music to Manage Your Mind, Body and Mood*. She suggests:

Try Latin music, or music with a lively, steady beat to energize.

Gregorian chants may relax. They are soothing and simple.

Beethoven's "Ode to Joy" will lift your heart. It begins slowly but moves toward a glorious and victorious ending.

The stormy, tragic tones of a Tchaikovsky piano concerto may help tears flow so you can release pent up emotions.

The methodical pace of Vivaldi's "The Four Seasons" is good for focus and concentration.

Listen to the beautiful sounds all around you.

Wine and music gladden the heart...The flute and the harp make sweet melody. (Sirach 40:20,21)

Father God, teach me to use music, meditation and prayer rather than relying on harmful habits.

I Think I Can

Dorothy James was young and poor, but she knew that her son, Stanford, was different. Even before he was diagnosed with autism, she "raised a fuss until he got transferred to a school that did right by him."

Stanford was fascinated by trains, and Dorothy took advantage of that interest. Together they rode back and forth on Chicago's trains. The conductors even knew them by name.

With Dorothy's encouragement, Stanford eventually graduated from high school. Today, despite his difficulties, he is the family's main breadwinner, a customer service representative for Chicago's Regional Transportation Authority. He relies on both computers and his vast personal knowledge of the city's train system.

In 1997 Stanford was named Employee of the Year.

"Stanford, you are the best man who can do everything," he tells himself when he solves a particularly difficult problem for a customer.

The Lord...confirms a mother's right over her children. (Sirach 3:2)

Loving Father, You create infinitely greater possibilities for us than we can imagine.

Children as Leaders

When a Catholic Bishop in Sumatra, Indonesia, Anicetus Sinaga, visited one of the communities, he was astounded to learn that 217 candidates for Baptism awaited him. He was even more amazed to discover that two young girls were responsible.

Every week, older children led younger ones in the Sunday service the community leader told the Bishop. And his two daughters, the leader noted, would "sing and pray, summarizing the readings and dramatizing the Gospel. ...Many children join them. When those children go home, these are the ones who invite their parents to church. Some 75 families became Roman Catholics in just this way!"

The experience reminded Bishop Sinaga that he, too, had converted his parents, and younger brothers and sisters, when he was a young seminarian.

Every believer of any age can bring relatives and friends to faith–if not by words, then by actions.

(The jailer) and his entire family were baptized without delay. (Acts 16:33)

You have called me, Lord, to tell the world about You.

Carrying God On the Job

Mary Ann Howard, a Beaumont, Texas, postal worker dreaded going to work on Mondays. In church on Sundays she was fine, but her sense of peace and happiness was tough to maintain on the job because of a difficult supervisor.

Then, walking her route one day, she became a hero. A woman ran out of her house carrying her infant and screaming, "My baby's not breathing!" Howard started mouth-to-mouth resuscitation as she prayed for help. Just as an emergency crew arrived, the infant opened her eyes.

When Mary Ann Howard returned to the post office, she no longer felt powerless. While she couldn't change her supervisor she knew she could change herself and her way of dealing with problems. And she determined not just to seek God on Sundays, but also to carry Him on her route each day, "as He carries me."

Let God carry you.

I led them with cords of human kindness, with bands of love. (Hosea 11:4)

Lord, be with me all the moments of my life.

Love is An Action

Everyday, John Stark, 91, remembers a few simple things: that millions of Americans go hungry, millions of Americans are homeless, and millions of Americans need help.

A volunteer at the Quincy Crisis Center in Quincy, Massachusetts, Stark helps feed between 30 and 80 people on any given day. Like other elderly volunteers at the Center, helping the homeless brings meaning and purpose to his life–an expression of his belief that Christians should care about all helpless, homeless and hungry people.

Whether he's serving meals, scrubbing pots or cleaning up the Center to prepare for the next day, Stark is putting his beliefs in action. How can you put your values and beliefs to work in the service of others?

Like good stewards...serve one another with whatever gift each of you has received.
(1 Peter 4:10)

Holy Spirit, Jesus taught us the true meaning of service. With Your guidance, we pray for the character and strength to emulate Him.

Camel Logic

Ever wondered how to control a runaway camel? Probably not. Yet, according to the authors of *The Worst Case Scenario Survival Handbook,* you can master the four steps necessary to corralling an unruly dromedary:

Hang onto the reins, but don't pull back on them too hard.

Pull the reins to one side and make the camel run in a circle. Basically, don't fight the animal.

If the camel has nose reins, just hang on tightly.

Hold on until the camel stops. It will eventually sit down when it grows tired.

One could apply these guidelines to any obstacle in life. Don't force things to happen. Work with others. Wait out a bad situation.

The answer to life is to "let go and let God."

Cast your burden on the Lord. (Psalm 55:22)

Father, help me depend on You and not try to go it alone.

A Floating House of Hope

Jerry Rouleau, a housing-industry consultant, dreamed up a novel way to raise funds for cancer awareness. To honor his late wife, Jan, who died of lung cancer in 1999, Rouleau constructed a state-of-the-art, seven-room, 3100-square-foot house on a barge.

Rouleau's plan is to have tugboats tow the 150 ft.-by-60 ft. barge down the eastern seaboard, from New Hampshire to Virginia. Along the way, the waterborne house will dock in seven cities, and Rouleau expects upwards of 250,000 people to pay $10 each to tour the home. Eventually, the home will be auctioned off for an estimated $500,000.

"I thought he was crazy," said Rouleau's sister-in-law. "But as he talked more about it I thought, 'He's going to do it.' And now, by God, he's done it."

Big dreams can produce big results. Act on your dreams.

Love...bears all things...hopes all things, endures all things. (1 Corinthians 13:7)

Lord and Maker, inspire me to think big when confronting problems.

Organizing Your Desk

If you're starting to feel overwhelmed by the mail that keeps piling up on your desk, perhaps it's time for an organizing system. Here are some steps to free your desk of paper:

- Separate all the papers on your desk into four stacks: "Do right now;" "important;" "interesting," "recycle."
- Put as many items as possible into the "interesting" or "recycle" stacks.
- Do the "do right now" stack when you're focused and ready.
- Take care of the "important" stack for a change of pace.
- Attend to the "interesting" stack when you need time to regroup.
- Try to make the system a habit.

When we set out to improve things one simple step at a time, the tasks at hand don't seem quite so daunting.

**Prosper for us the work of our hands.
(Psalm 90:17)**

Father, help me be in command of my daily work.

Blossom of Snow

Have you ever seen a snow buttercup blooming beneath a thin sheet of ice?

These delicate blossoms gather up enough energy from the few dim rays of sun which manage to reach through the snow to actually produce flowers.

The first time Peter Marchand saw one in bloom he was amazed. "From under the granular crust of a subalpine snowfield sprang forth life as tender and fresh as a butterfly's newly unfolded wings," he wrote.

Marchand, author of *Life in the Cold*, examines plants and growth through the eyes of a scientist. He understands how plants get energy from reserve carbohydrates. "In the race to reproduce, these plants can't wait for the snow to melt," he adds.

Perhaps your heart knows what it's like to live through winter, touched only by the feeblest rays of sun. Seek the light of God and you will find it.

My flesh and my heart may fail, but God is the strength of my heart and my portion forever. (Psalm 73:26)

Help us to build reserves through prayer, Lord, that we may have faith even in the dark of winter.

Emotional Maturity

How can we promote mental health? It helps to know something about what emotional maturity entails.

Dr. William Menninger, of the noted Menninger Institute in Topeka, Kansas, gives these criteria of emotional maturity:

1. The ability to deal with reality constructively.

2. The capacity to adapt to change.

3. The ability to find more satisfaction in giving than receiving.

4. The capacity to relate to other people in a consistent manner with mutual satisfaction and helpfulness.

5. The ability to direct one's instinctive hostile energy into creative and constructive outlets.

6. The capacity to love.

Obviously, each of these is important, but surely "the capacity to love" is special.

Bless the God of all...who fosters our growth from birth...according to His mercy.
(Sirach 50:22)

Guide me, Lord, as I grow in emotional health. Help me foster it in others through and in Your love.

Women Ski into History

As youngsters, teachers Ann Bancroft and Liv Arnesen had been captivated by tales of the survival of Sir Ernest Shackleton's Antarctic expedition (1914–1916) under the most extreme conditions.

They fulfilled their dream and made history in February, 2001, when they became the first women to ski across the Antarctic. During their arduous 1700 mile, three-month journey, Bancroft and Arnesen endured altitude fatigue and temperatures averaging 20 degrees below zero and winds gusting up to 50 mph.

Other than two days spent with researchers at the South Pole, their contact with the outside world was primarily through an Internet site. It was monitored by millions of children worldwide. "Our classroom is bigger now," said Bancroft.

These intrepid women, like the many explorers who went before them, can inspire you to pursue your dreams–no matter what others may think of those dreams.

Be courageous and valiant. (2 Samuel 13:28)

Lord, with Your help I can live my dreams and reach my goals.

Grass Roots Growth

Because she had been taught to be nice to everybody, "it was hard to stand up to politicians and tell them what we wanted," says Virginia Ramirez.

But she learned to tell government officials what her San Antonio neighborhood needed and held them accountable for fulfilling their promises. Ms. Ramirez joined a local volunteer group, COPS (Communities Organized for Public Services) over 20 years ago and helped it grow by leaps and bounds.

Since then, COPS has attracted about a billion dollars in public and private investment for basics such as sidewalks and storm drains. And Ramirez, a self-described traditional Hispanic wife and mother, obtained her GED and college degree. She also learned to research, negotiate, articulate and channel her anger.

She says, "I thought about how...with other people you can change things."

What can you and your neighbors do for the good of your community?

A woman who fears the Lord is to be praised. (Proverbs 31:30)

Give me the courage to make changes, Father of heaven and earth.

Eating Nothing, Saying Something

From the Prophets to Jesus and Mohammed to Gandhi and Cesar Chavez, fasting from food to make a moral statement has a long history.

Lately, "there's been a definite increase in fasting," said Kim Bobo, executive director of the National Interfaith Committee for Worker Justice. "As people of faith seek increasingly to struggle for justice in this time of abundance, it's a natural outgrowth that fasting would be something they do."

People often fast in solidarity with those who suffer. For instance, not everyone reaps a decent share in the global economy. "Those not participating cannot speak for themselves," said the Roman Catholic bishop of Albany, Howard Hubbard. "We have to be a voice for the voiceless."

The ability to fast from food also depends on one's health, and there are other effective, if less dramatic, ways to highlight injustices. Whatever your method, speak up for peace and justice.

Prayer with fasting is good, but better than both is almsgiving with righteousness. (Tobit 12:8)

Holy Spirit, help us fast from acquisitiveness and ostentation.

Credit Desire

What seems like an endless limit on credit cards can be used up with astonishing speed. In the end, many have little to show for their indebtedness except a tremendous financial burden.

Kelly Schmid was 17 when her mother gave her a credit card for emergency use. While at college, Kelly turned to plastic for everything from textbooks to parking tickets. Soon she found herself using the card to eat out or to purchase extra clothes.

Her mom paid the bills, so Kelly was able to secure additional cards on her own. By age 22, she had run up nearly $10,000 in debt on ten different cards. Today, Kelly and her mom are paying off the debt but mom keeps the cards.

"It's ironic," Kelly admits. She used the charge cards as a way to feel free from her parents, but is now more indebted to them than ever. That's a valuable–if expensive–lesson.

One who pursues money will be led astray by it. Many have come to ruin because of gold...It is a stumbling block to those who are avid for it. (Sirach 31:5-6,7)

Make us brave enough, God, to ask for help when we need it.

Simple Message, Enormous Impact

Ernest Thompson Seton was a prolific writer who ardently believed that nature is a very good thing. He authored some 60 books and nearly 400 magazine articles and short stories during the latter part of the 19th century and early part of the 20th.

A self-trained biologist, Seton concentrated on birds and mammals, their habits and habitats, and why they should be cherished and protected. His book, *Wild Animals I Have Known,* was published in 1898 and has remained in print ever since.

Seton's message about the importance of nature and wildlife was simple, but some say no one did more than he did to promote that indisputably true idea.

What are the basic values and beliefs that define you? Try listing the core values by which you try to live. It could help you keep your priorities in focus.

Where your treasure is, there your heart will be also. (Matthew 6:21)

Lord Jesus, help me simplify my life. Help me weed out the distractions that take my focus off You.

Learning from Tough Times

Well-known Christian author and apologist C.S. Lewis once labeled pain "God's megaphone." God does seem to get our attention when we're in physical or emotional pain; when we want to shout, "Why me, God?"

Virelle Kidder learned firsthand about pain and patience when she slipped and fell, injuring two disks in her back. As she recovered sitting in a neck traction device and feeling sidelined, she wondered what God was trying to teach her

During those 15 months Kidder, never a patient person, had to learn to sit still and be quiet. Later, she realized that the period of healing led her to become a writer.

Virelle Kidder says, "It was a significant turning point in my life when I realized God's more interested in who I become than in what I do."

If we let it, our suffering may open the door to a new and deeper spiritual awareness.

For God alone my soul waits in silence, for my hope is from Him. He alone is my rock and my salvation, my fortress...my deliverance and my honor. (Psalm 62:5-6,7)

Gentle my soul, calm my mind, open my whole being to Your sweet whisper, Holy Spirit.

A Solution to Job Problems?

Without a doubt, problems are a part of work. What's not always clear is whether the real problem at any given time is us. Based on decades of marketplace experience writer Verla Gilmor offers these problem-solving tips:

- Identify the real problem. She once created a new project to please her supervisor and ended up angry at not having any help with the extra work. The real problem? She needed affirmation but couldn't ask for it.

- Take charge of your attitude. Complaining is pointless. If change is truly possible, offer a solution.

- Detach from the problem. Not everything is personal.

- Live in the present.

Every life and every day has problems. We need to deal with them, but most of all, we need to trust God.

We are ambassadors for Christ, since God is making His appeal through us.
(2 Corinthians 5:20)

Holy Wisdom, keep us optimistic in the face of difficulties.

"Equal To My Life"

As her husband, world-famous aviator Charles Lindbergh, lay dying, Anne Morrow Lindbergh told their daughter, Reeve, "Don't worry about me. I'm equal to my life." When her mother died 27 years later, Reeve thought, "What a life it was and she was equal to it."

A pilot, author, and mother of six children, Anne Morrow Lindbergh met her famous husband after his 1927 transatlantic flight. They gained worldwide attention both for their flying and for her first book, *North to the Orient.* Then their son, Charles Jr., was kidnapped and later found dead. Believing their fame had helped to kill their son, they tried to live quietly.

Still, 11 more books including, *A Gift from the Sea,* followed between 1932 and 1974.

We, too, have tribulations and our own versions of "fame and fortune." God's grace and our character get us through it all.

Blessed be the Lord...my rock and my fortress, my stronghold...my shield. (Psalm 144:1,2)

Give me Your own courage, Mighty Lord.

Eliminating a Lethal Disease

Dr. Brian Druker always dreamed about making a difference. With the STI-571 pill, which targets chronic myelogenous leukemia, or CML, it appears he has done just that.

As a young oncologist, Druker dreaded telling patients there was nothing more he could do for them; ultimately writing condolence letters to their families. He vowed to do better and eventually developed a drug that would target and destroy cancer cells.

Glivec, as STI-571 has been labeled, destroys a protein that causes the rampant overproduction of white blood cells. After six months of Glivec 31, CML patients went into remission. "It's truly a miracle pill," said one.

Dr. Druker insists his real reward is his office bulletin board displaying pictures of surviving patients. "That's what it's all about," says Druker. "...knowing I've done good."

Can you say the same?

To each is given the manifestation of the Spirit for the common good. (1 Corinthians 12:7)

May each of us strive to make a positive difference, Holy One.

Amazing Animal Kingdom

The animal world never ceases to amaze.

Take toads and frogs. Chemists analyzing secretions on their skin have found anesthetics, hallucinogens and neurotoxins.

Then, there are dolphins. Even at bedtime, they are only half asleep. Deep sleep occurs only in one brain hemisphere at a time. They sleep with one eye open, maintaining visual contact with the rest of their school.

Consider killer whales. Orca cooperate with each other to orchestrate the capture of prey. They get together and swim around and under a school of herring in a coordinated fashion. In so doing, they force the smaller fish into a "ball" near the water's surface. Once the herring are handy, the whales slap them with their huge tails and proceed to eat the stunned creatures.

These behavioral realities are not always attractive; but the creatures with whom we share the Earth are truly beautiful creatures of God.

God created the great sea monsters and every living creature...with which the waters swarm. (Genesis 1:21)

Encourage us to repair the damage we have done to the oceans and the land, Creator.

A Child of Invention

Three years ago, Spencer Whale, then just six, was given a school project and decided it would have a medical theme. He visited a children's hospital in his native Pittsburgh to do research, and found that it was difficult for kids to move with an IV pole.

Spencer's solution? Attach the IV pole to a child's pedal car. This way, kids could move around freely–and perhaps take their mind off their health problems; maybe even enjoy, just a little bit, the time that they had to spend in the hospital.

Recently Spencer spent time at Winthrop University's Cancer Center for Kids, making new friends and seeing his invention in use. "When I see these kids, I realize they're really just like me, but they're sick," Spencer said, adding that he was grateful he could see them smile.

Try to help someone today.

Wisdom...is first pure, then peaceable, gentle, willing to yield, full of mercy and good fruits. (James 3:17)

I cry out to You, Father, answer my prayer; show me Your mercy.

Bar None

Walk into California's overcrowded Chuckawalla Valley State Prison and you'll find 3,700 men, many of whom are serving life sentences. You'll probably also find volunteer Kim G., a choreographer using dance, yoga, and storytelling in workshops.

Working with small groups, she asks prisoners to remain in class only if they will participate fully. Kim starts her sessions with innocuous questions.

"What did you have for lunch today?" she might ask. After a few answers, she asks, "Now tell me what you wish you had for lunch today!" Before long her students are rapping with songs about bland sack lunches and the longed-for muffins, cake or jam on toast.

Kim knows rehabilitation requires much more than she can offer. "But one thing I can do is pull them into the present moment," she says. "And, at least for that moment, I hope it's healing."

Everyone needs healing some time, just as everyone needs a second chance.

Remember those who are in prison. (Hebrews 13:3)

Let us look overwhelming odds in the face, Lord, and do what we can.

Bird Man of New Jersey

Three years ago, Pete Dunne decided to get selfish. "I spend all of my time working; I'm not spending the time enjoying," he thought.

So Dunne left his office job, moved to Cumberland County in his native New Jersey—and now makes a living as a "birder" at the Cape May Bird Observatory.

Dunne grew up in rural Morris County where his home was surrounded by extensive woods—and lots of birds. Another child got him interested in bird-watching. "She was 9; I was 7," he recalls. "The only thing we knew about birds was that you had to get up early."

These days Dunne still gets up early, but has learned a lot more about our feathered friends. A vice president of the New Jersey Audubon Society, he has authored a number of books on the subject. "This is really rejuvenating," Dunne says of his passion for studying birds. "This is really a great charge in the morning."

Embrace your life, each and every morning!

Look at the birds of the air; they neither sow nor reap nor gather into barns, and yet your heavenly Father feeds them. (Matthew 6:26)

Lift me up, Father, when I am weary. Refresh me with Your life and love.

Yes You Can!

Are you too busy to volunteer? Think again.

"Charities are keenly aware of how many good causes tug at our schedules," says *Good Housekeeping* magazine, "and they're willing to be flexible with volunteers."

Here are some suggestions for those who have a limited amount of time to volunteer. If your schedule would only permit one day per year, for instance, they suggested helping community organizations by planting flowers, picking up recyclables, or lending a hand with spring cleaning.

If one day each month seems manageable, they recommend helping at-risk kids by chaperoning outings or helping them explore careers through an after school program. Those who can give an hour on a weekly basis might volunteer to conduct tours at a local museum, visit elderly people in rehabilitation, or answer phones at a social service agency.

Everyone has something to give. Creativity is the key.

**A generous person will be enriched.
(Proverbs 11:25)**

Open my mind to new ideas, Lord, and let me embrace them enthusiastically.

A Call to Action

Leviticus 19:14 tells us, "You shall not...put a stumbling block before the blind." Well, who would do that? Certainly, no decent person would intentionally try to harm someone, least of all someone physically challenged.

Despite our intentions, we all, at one time or another, have put a stumbling block before another. We are accountable for our actions and, likewise, for what we fail to do. We do this when we:

- Ignore the plight of the poor
- Enable an addiction
- Promote unhealthy beauty standards
- Tolerate violence
- Close our eyes to injustice

There are many kinds of blindness, and it's up to us to protect the vulnerable, encourage the young, promote peace and foster understanding.

You shall not steal...deal falsely...lie...defraud your neighbor...keep...the wages of a laborer... revile the deaf or put a stumbling block before the blind. (Leviticus 19:11,13,14)

Open our eyes, King of Justice and Peace, that we may see Your path and follow Your example.

What's In a Word?

Who knows where the phrases "hot dog" and "Murphy's law" came from? Barry Popik, that's who.

This part-time New York City judge is a full-time word detective, a restless genius of American etymology who spends his off-hours unearthing the past of American English. Popik distributes the results of his research over the Internet through the American Dialect Society. He has posted the meaning of 1,000 words and phrases.

"There's no question that Barry is one of the greatest researchers alive," says Jesse Sheidlower, principal North American editor for the *Oxford English Dictionary*. It was Popik, for example, who discovered that New York was first called the "Big Apple" by 1920s horse-racing insiders, who considered the city the top racing venue.

His quest these days: tracking down the origin of "the whole nine yards." "Give me a month," says Popik.

Develop your interests. You can't tell just how far they'll take you.

Now you are speaking plainly, not in any figure of speech! (John 16:29)

I offer You this prayer of thanksgiving, Master, for You are the source of all good things.

Workday Spirituality

People change jobs for many reasons, including more money, improved benefits and new challenges. A growing number of men and women are adding spirituality to that list.

Bill Carver, author of *The Job Hunter's Spiritual Companion*, believes "it's important that we grant ourselves the freedom to live our unique lives without the pressure of meeting externally imposed expectations."

Richard McGarry was one worker who felt the urge to make a change. After more than thirty years with a lucrative job in sales, he wanted to pursue his "heart's desire," to be a teacher. So, with the support of his wife and much prayer, he earned a degree and took a job as a religious education teacher at a local high school. "The spiritual is in all areas of my life," McGarry now says.

Spirituality is not a sometime thing. Whatever you do, keep your sights on God. Ultimately, He is your heart's desire.

My soul thirsts for You; my flesh faints for You...So I have looked upon You in the sanctuary. (Psalm 63:1,2)

Holy Trinity, One God, may my work be Your work.

Busy? Take Time Out for Tea!

Jamien Morehouse gave an unusual tea party in 1986.

She decided to invite friends and acquaintances to join her for tea on March 20th–the vernal equinox. But rather than getting together, she sent two tea bags to a hundred women and asked them to invite a friend to join them at 4 o'clock on that day to commit themselves "to a springtime of rejuvenation and good humor, and a lifetime of peace."

Morehouse, who enjoyed life as an artist, community activist, wife, and mother of four sons in Rockport, Maine, died of cancer in 1999. But her tradition continues.

At times, life becomes hectic. We become consumed trying to solve problems, meet deadlines, and juggle activities. Take time out for yourself occasionally–and be sure to invite a friend to join you.

I trust in You, O Lord; I say, "You are my God." My times are in Your Hand. (Psalm 31:14-15)

Dear God, take us into Your arms and show us the beauty of this earth and the time You give us.

A Different Kind of Spring Break

Carrie Haslett, a Trinity College senior, is one of countless students who decided not to "party hearty" during Spring break, but rather to do something constructive for others.

The Massachusetts native took part in Habitat for Humanity's collegiate challenge. It entails thousands of volunteers building houses for the poor throughout the country and the world. Sawing, hammering, painting, their contribution is very hands-on.

"This feels so good," said Haslett, "to see the fruits of your labor so immediately is gratifying. People here care more about doing something meaningful than...how good their tan is."

It's not that these student volunteers are all work and no play. In fact, says Haslett, "Don't get me wrong, I'm trying to get the tan, too." But she is happy to be doing something practical for others in need.

Work and play. Doing good and relaxing. The challenge: balance.

**Good works...cannot remain hidden.
(1 Timothy 5:25)**

Teach us, Holy Spirit, to balance the many equally worthwhile, even necessary, elements of our lives.

Adult Allowances

Remember as children how you got an allowance? As parents and grandparents you probably give allowances to–and make allowances for–children. Yet as an adult you may not often extend that generosity toward yourself. Amidst all the *musts* and *shoulds* of life, how about incorporating some "adult allowances?"

You are *allowed* to follow your dream.

You are *allowed* to laugh and have fun.

You are *allowed* to have time for yourself.

You are *allowed* to be creative.

You are *allowed* to have a bad day.

You are *allowed* to make mistakes.

You are *allowed* to change your mind.

You are *allowed* not to know all the answers.

That last one is key. There is only One who has all the answers. Give yourself a break today.

What are human beings that you are mindful of them...You have made them a little lower than God. (Psalm 8:4,5)

When inhuman and ungodly perfectionism strikes, Savior, deliver us.

Portraits in Time

Tastes in art change. Yet some styles and forms are popular for centuries. The miniature is one of the latter.

The word itself comes from the Latin *minium* for the red lead ink originally used. The English use of miniature meaning something small actually comes from these tiny portraits. Painted on ivory, vellum, porcelain or enamel, they reached the height of their appeal from the mid-17th through 19th centuries. Depicting clear images of the subject on a surface only about three inches high required a skillful technique.

The advent of less costly and time-consuming photography diminished the miniature's appeal, though they are still prized by collectors. $1.2 million was paid for a two inch portrait of George Washington–per square inch that's the highest price ever paid for a work of art.

What is the true worth of all you hold dear? Do you value your family, your good character and kind deeds? You should.

A good name is to be chosen rather than great riches. (Proverbs 22:1)

Carpenter of Nazareth, help me appreciate the Creator's wondrous gifts.

Revolutionary Remedy

Dr. Francesca Gany insists she is a shy person. "If I had to sell you a pair of shoes, I couldn't do it."

Yet she is on a mission to make the American health-care system more responsive to the foreign born. To that end, Dr. Gany has even conducted a long distance ceremony with the help of a healer in Senegal for a patient who would not otherwise accept American medicine.

She has improved immigrant accessibility to state programs and launched a task force at NYU's School of Medicine. The result has been a greatly improved sensitivity to beliefs of other cultures, a key to the healing process.

"My experience has made me believe you have to go out there," she observes, "and in your own minor, quiet way, create a little bit of a revolution."

Create your own revolution by helping your neighbors.

God, the Lord, is my strength; He makes my feet like the feet of a deer, and makes me tread upon the heights. (Habakkuk 3:19)

Let us answer Your call to ignore obstacles and focus on possibilities, Lord.

The Protective Power of Prayer

Roberta Messner, nurse and chronic-pain sufferer, was feeling so discouraged that she cancelled an appointment with yet another specialist. Nothing will help, she figured. "I'd even stopped praying about it," she recalls.

Then, at a health fair, she recommended that an elderly man get a flu shot. He scoffed, saying that his wife had gotten one the previous winter and had had a severe case of the flu.

Later, complaining to a colleague about "some people's stubbornness" when it comes to their best interest, she realized that she was being just as stubborn. "I had cancelled my appointment with a new doctor."

Messner rescheduled her appointment. She also realized that prayer offers protection against doubt, fear and hopelessness. "I still recommend flu shots to patients," she says, "but I also… remember…the power of prayer."

Prayer is always powerful.

Pray to your Father who is in secret; and your Father who sees in secret will reward you. (Matthew 6:6)

Lord, remind us that prayer protects us and gives us hope.

Keeping up with Changes

Biology education isn't like it used to be, if anything is. But the study of life has gone through major changes that show no sign of letting up.

How are teachers coping? Some are pulling out their hair.

They literally pull out strands of their own hair to study DNA isolation procedures while attending the Dolan DNA Learning Center at New York's Cold Spring Harbor Laboratory.

"When I started teaching in 1969, we did our march through the phyla," said Marilyn Havlik, chairwoman of a high school science department. "Now I don't teach any animal systems. The Chicago curriculum includes genetics, evolution, ecology and cell structure."

On-going education helps teachers improve their skill so that they can in turn skillfully guide students through rapid changes in education and in life.

Think about the way you handle the changes that are a normal part of your life.

I the Lord do not change; therefore you...have not perished. (Malachi 3:6)

God, help us cope with the unchanging reality of change.

Surviving Survival

The twin-engine turboprop plane carrying Bob Gault's family crash-landed on Michigan's Beaver Island. The pilots died.

Gault's wife Mirth, daughter Emma and sons Adam and Alec survived the 15-hour wait for rescue. Mrs. Gault told the children that they had to be strong to get back to their dad. Meanwhile, Adam unbelted himself from the wreckage and rushed his brother out of the plane. Then he helped his mother free Emma, who was injured and trapped in her seat.

Meanwhile, a local pilot braved the weather to help in the search. In 30 minutes he had spotted the fuselage, with Mirth Gault atop it waving a life preserver. He called in a Coast Guard chopper to rescue the family.

"Another half-hour," said Bob Gault when he was reunited with his family, "and we wouldn't have found them until spring. ...You never know what you have until it's gone."

Appreciate God's gift of your family and friends.

Love one another with mutual affection. (Romans 12:10)

Help us cherish our families, Father of all.

Hope Is a Meadow

At the same time that two-year-old Keri was placed in foster care after extreme neglect, Elmer and Marjorie Davis were deep in retirement boredom. "She didn't talk at all," recalls her foster mother.

Today Elmer and Marjorie have never been busier and you won't find a more talkative child than Keri.

What made the difference? Hope Meadows, a community founded by Brenda Krause Eheart in Rantoul, Illinois, that pairs kids who need parents with parents who need kids.

"You have these two marginalized groups— foster kids...and seniors," Eheart explains. "Here, they're meeting each other's needs."

Eheart's one-of-a-kind neighborhood of 47 foster, adopted and biological kids and 56 surrogate grandparents is working. Just ask Elmer Davis. "Here, we're needed," he offers. "Boy, are we needed."

Find the person who needs you. Share yourself.

Pay to all what is due them...respect to whom respect is due, honor to whom honor is due. (Romans 13:7)

Father, show me what to do this day, so that others may experience Your love.

How to Find Happiness

What does it take to make us happy? Is it wealth, power, social relationships?

Contrary to popular opinion, increasing pleasure and decreasing pain won't lead to happiness, according to Steven Reiss, Ph.D. Reiss distinguishes two types of happiness, feel-good and value-based. Feel-good, such as enjoying a good laugh or a good party, doesn't last.

But happiness based on living our lives in accord with the values most important to us is lasting. Decide what you value, for instance, family, status, honor, idealism, and act accordingly.

This will provide "a sense that our lives have meaning and fulfill some larger purpose. It represents a spiritual source of satisfaction, stemming from our deeper purpose and values," said Dr. Reiss.

"Wealthy people are not necessarily happy, and poor people are not necessarily unhappy. Values, not pleasure, are what bring true happiness."

Consider all that makes you happy.

Learn where there is wisdom...strength... understanding. (Baruch 3:14)

Set my intellect and heart to value what You do, Savior.

Recipe for Comfort

"Cooking is almost always a mood-altering experience: more calming than yoga, less risky than drugs."

That's the assessment of Regina Schrambling writing in *The New York Times*. "The food is not really the thing," she says. "It's the making of it that gets you through a bad time."

For Schrambling, the comfort comes from the fact that cooking engages the senses–and can soothe them as well. "Sometimes it just feels calming to know that a cake needs exactly one teaspoon of salt and no less than a half pound of butter," she explains.

There is also the sense of accomplishment. "When you're all finished, you have something to show for the time and effort: a loaf of bread, a batch of cookies, a pot of stew," Schrambling says. "Cooking when you have no hope is sometimes just what you need to get to a better place."

Seek God's comfort in a kitchen, a church, or wherever you happen to be.

If we hope for what we do not see, we wait for it with patience. (Romans 8:25)

Father, lift me up when I have fallen into despair.

Advocate for Patients

Nancy Davenport-Ennis' friend Cheryl Grimmel went through a bone marrow transplant. Four days before the surgery, Grimmel's insurance company told her it would not cover the $200,000 cost for the experimental treatment. Grimmel was plagued by debt for her last three-and-a-half years of life.

Davenport-Ennis, herself a breast cancer survivor, thought that no one should have to suffer as had her friend, so she developed a business plan for *The Patient Advocate Foundation (PAF)*. Its goal: to help patients handle denied insurance claims and other major problems that result from a serious illness.

Today, the *PAF* helps thousands of patients, and Nancy Davenport-Ennis spends most of her time lobbying Congress for better health plans. Inspired and motivated by a friend's life and death, she has made her life's work helping those who are at their wit's end and in desperate need of assistance.

Make your life count for something.

Act with justice and righteousness. (Jeremiah 22:3)

If there is a wrong, show me how to right it, Jesus.

The Effect of Laughter

According to the *Journal of the American Medical Association (JAMA)*, laughter's effect on body chemistry can help the immune system and ease allergies. In other words, a hearty laugh is healthful. Bring more amusement into your life by trying the following:

- Hone your sense of humor: read the funny papers, go to comedy clubs, rent videos of classic comedies to expand your comic vision.
- Get a little help from the pros: consider joining a laughter club, where participants are led through exercises that encourage playfulness, fun and mental balance.
- Spread the joy by jotting down jokes or stories you want to remember. Share these with co-workers.
- Stay positive. The therapeutic power of laughter can keep us healthy.

Laughter can energize and renew us. Give in to a heartfelt laugh today.

He will yet fill your mouth with laughter, and your lips with shouts of joy. (Job 8:21)

May joy and laughter fill our lives, Lord Jesus.

Three Strikes, You're In

"Joe, this is embarrassing because I don't like to ask for help, but…"

"My pride and self-confidence have completely disappeared. I stay in the house almost every day–usually in my pajamas."

"My (prosthetic) legs are in the making. I went for a fitting and for the first time since July I walked and what a thrill that was."

The letter writers are retired athletes who played on Major League baseball teams in the era before multimillion-dollar contracts. Now, down on their luck, they seek help from Joe Garagiola, sportscaster, former player and TV personality, for everything from cancer surgery and alcohol rehabilitation to funeral expenses for a wife.

As a major supporter and spokesman for BAT, the Baseball Assistance Team, Garagiola has helped it raise millions of dollars. Other well-known players also help the cause. Because of these efforts, the former athletes and their families have renewed hope.

Restoring hope to the despairing is a most humane thing.

Hope does not disappoint us. (Romans 5:5)

Open our hearts and minds to others' needs, Father.

The Cost of Staying Connected

We human beings are social beings. What can be bad about staying connected to others?

Well, at times it seems we're becoming divided between those who love cell phones and those who hate those who love them! Actually, what they generally hate is the often loud and inane one-sided conversations.

The New York Times printed what some call "cell yell" and others call conversation. Most people can probably come up with their own selections.

Hi, how are you? Yes, sweetheart. Can you hear me? Can you HEAR me? Tell him to pick me up on the 6:48. Can you HEAR me?

We all want to be heard—even those without cell phones. But, as in other areas of life, a little courtesy goes a long way.

Let your speech always be gracious...so that you may know how...to answer everyone. (Colossians 4:6)

Inspire us to use Your gift of speech with love and in love, Eternal Father.

The Progress of Science

Benjamin Franklin, one of the foremost scientists and "natural philosophers" of the 18th century, was also a printer, diplomat and architect of our Declaration of Independence. His experiments with electricity helped pave the way for great advances later on.

The first American to make an aerial voyage, John Jeffries, carried a flight barometer thought to be the world's oldest when he crossed the English Channel in a balloon in 1785. John Winthrop, a prominent mathematician and astronomer, used a London-made telescope whose optical design had been introduced in 1663.

These and countless scientists and researchers over the centuries gained knowledge despite the use of primitive and rudimentary tools.

Alan Fern, director of the National Portrait Gallery in Washington, D.C., noted, "the care with which" they did their "studies, documented their findings, and shared the results."

Carefulness, meticulous documentation and sharing are keys to discovery and learning.

Be careful then how you live. (Ephesians 5:15)

Thank You for our willingness to wonder, Maker of all.

The Healing Power of Forgiveness

"It is terribly hard to forgive those who have hurt us so powerfully. I know from my own experience, however, that forgiveness is the only response that will bring an end to the pain and a healing to the heart."

In a letter reprinted by June O'Connor, Ph.D., in her *Catholic Digest* column, one former child-abuse victim comforted and advised another letter writer about the importance and ultimate solace of forgiveness.

"From one survivor to another, I want you to know that forgiveness is not a feeling. Forgiveness is a choice...It is true that the memories may never disappear entirely, but I have found that after choosing to forgive the person who has done harm, the memories lose their power and the pain lessens."

Offering forgiveness to someone who has hurt you may be one of the most healing things you can do for yourself.

Be kind to one another, tenderhearted, forgiving one another as God in Christ has forgiven you. (Ephesians 4:32)

Please help me, God, to forgive those who have hurt me, and as importantly, to ask for forgiveness, when necessary.

Influencing Human Relations

Life can be difficult at times. In our crowded and stressful world, maintaining positive dealings with everyone we come in contact with can be a real challenge. Here are a few simple suggestions for fostering more amicable relations:

- Smile at people.
- Speak to them.
- Call people by name.
- Be cordial.
- Have a genuine interest in others.
- Be generous with praise.
- Be considerate of the feelings of others.
- Be alert to give service.

Incorporate these simple practices and watch as you and your relationships improve and grow.

Happy is the one who finds a friend. (Sirach 25:9)

Smile on and speak to me this day, Lord and Giver.

A Root of Evil–If We Let It Be

Money and faith are often seen as rivals. After all, it's a common saying that money is the root of all evil. But money can be positive if handled properly and treated as the tool it is and not worshipped as the god it isn't.

Jim Auer, an English and religion teacher, wrote in the *St. Anthony Messenger* that the best way to view money is as a gift, but a dangerous one. Auer also notes that unlike the thanks we accord to God for other things we receive, we seldom give thanks for money. We should, he writes, because money is a gift that enables us to acquire things...and do good for others.

St. Paul reminds us that "the love of money is a root of all kinds of evil" (1 Timothy 6:10). It's our responsibility to use money, or any other gift, well–not to love it for its own sake.

Give me neither poverty nor riches; feed me with the food that I need, or I shall be full, and deny You...or I shall be poor, and steal. (Proverbs 30:8-9)

Teach us, Holy Wisdom, to use our material resources wisely and justly.

Dealing with Kids and Guilt

Psychology professor June Tangney of George Mason University believes that "kids who feel guilt are tuned in to the consequences of their actions and want to fix the situation."

She suggests that parents help children understand the effects of their wrongdoing without shaming them: "Notice how your kids react when they've been scolded. Shame-prone kids focus more on themselves...respond with withdrawal or anger. When children are angry, it's hard for them to recognize what the other person is feeling."

Parents should not encourage shame by saying, "You're mean." Instead say, "You just hit Mary. We don't do that. It hurt her." Adults also need to model good behavior. Apologize when you say something to your child in anger and later regret. Say, "I love you."

A parent's constructive response to children's misdeeds can help them deal with shame and guilt when it's appropriate and understand when it is not. That's important for us all to learn.

Do not judge, so that you may not be judged. (Matthew 7:1)

Help us be positive role models for children, Father.

Learning True Contentment

John Berry left a successful corporate career to join the Internet revolution. Soon, the Internet company for which he worked was acquired and his position was terminated. He lost his stock options in the process.

In the meantime, Berry's wife, an avid horsewoman, told him that riding was a form of therapy for her. Soon after, he bartered a deal with a stable. In exchange for riding lessons for his daughter, he and his family would take care of the stable's horses three days a week.

Berry found enormous satisfaction in working with horses; bringing them in from the field to their stalls provided him a quiet contentment. He experienced an immediate sense of accomplishment, a tangible sense of fulfillment.

John Berry discovered that being with his family and working with and experiencing the beauty and grace embodied in horses were invaluable gifts; gifts more important than stock options any day.

Seek joy in simple and satisfying moments.

Be content with what you have. (Hebrews 13:5)

I know that contentment is not found in material gain, Lord. Please don't let me forget it.

Rattling Around the House

Warm apple pie, well-worn sweaters, and big, comfortable porch swings. It's easy to romanticize all that home represents.

"But home isn't necessarily a neat and tidy place, physically or emotionally," freelance writer Molly Wolf says. She thinks home is in the friction.

"We do most of our best soul-work by rubbing up against each other's roughnesses, banging into elbows, getting necessarily rattled. Spiritual growth can be exhilarating and joyous... confusing, exhausting, and fractious."

Although Wolf loves her hometown, she describes it as a little scruffy, unfocused and perhaps apologetic. She writes, "God is here. All we have to do is to notice, to be aware of it, and God's love washes through and over the ordinariness...And then it becomes so easy to love this plainness, to see the beauty that shines softly through this shabbiness."

God is here.

In the beloved city He gave me a resting place and in Jerusalem was my domain. I took root in an honored people. (Sirach 24:11-12)

Teach us to embrace the ordinariness of life, Lord.

The Garbage Behind the Art

The lush peaks and valleys of the Blue Ridge Mountain community of Penland, North Carolina, are home to some of the nation's finest craft workshops–and to the former dump of Mitchell and Yancey Counties.

In fact, the two happily co-exist. A power project channels the methane gas from the dump into fuel for furnaces for glass blowers and metal workers as well as potters' kilns, saving the artists an estimated $1 million in energy costs during the 12 to 20 years the gas is expected to last. Glass blower John Geci pays from $200 to $350 a month, instead of an estimated $1,000.

Jon Ellenbogen, a potter, hopes the Penland project inspires others to do the same. "There are some 900 small landfills around the nation like ours," he said. "We're the perfect example of how individual talents can be pooled together for the greater good."

How often do we think about serving "the greater good?"

The gifts He gave were...to equip the saints for the work of ministry, for building up the body of Christ. (Ephesians 4:11,12)

Creator, Your ways are not ours. Help me to be led in Your ways this day–and to lead others to You.

We Speak Your Language

It's important to be understood and to understand.

In suburban New York, people with diverse ethnicities keep a link to their original homelands with news and talk programs broadcast in their own languages on several radio stations. For new residents with a limited command of English, radio is a lifeline.

"They need to adjust to the American way of life; that's why they're tuned to their radio 24/7," said Jouhard Nicolas, founder of Haitian Radio Verite. The ultimate goal is for newcomers to become full participants in the life of their new home, but "cultural bridges" help with the transition.

"At the beginning, I was afraid that no one would listen," said radio host Jola Naklicka. "(Now) people tell me it's so great that there's a Polish station. They miss their language, their country, everything."

Let's welcome new neighbors and help them fit in.

The whole earth had one language and the same words. (Genesis 11:1)

Grant courage to those who start new lives in new lands, Jesus.

The Palm Sunday Tradition

The palm fronds handed out on Palm Sunday are part of a lovely tradition which recalls the first Palm Sunday procession over two millennia ago.

Some people use those same palms to create beautiful art as an extension of the tradition and a way to enjoy time together practicing an age-old Christian tradition. Palm designs can be as tiny as a coin or as large as a framed picture. From just a few fronds, a skilled weaver can braid intricate designs, such as the crown of thorns. Some woven pieces are designed to adorn other objects of art. For many craftspeople, simply constructing an attractive cross is a sufficient reminder of God's love and presence.

The simplest things can be a source of joy. Consider ways you could enhance your joy by simplifying your life.

The great crowd...heard that Jesus was coming to Jerusalem. So they took branches of palm trees and went out to meet Him, shouting, "Hosanna! Blessed is the one who comes in the name of the Lord—the King of Israel!" (John 12:12-13)

Help me simplify my life, Lord God, so that I may remain focused on what matters.

Laughing All the Way at the Bank

At one 7 a.m. staff meeting, Bobbe White passed out an agenda that listed "stress reduction technique."

When that item came up, her 45 co-workers at a Quincy, Illinois, bank were shown a brief television news feature on laughter clubs in India. After that, White removed her blazer to reveal a "Laughter Tour" t-shirt and proclaimed herself a "certified laugh leader." She asked those present to stand up with her in a circle, leading them in breathing, stretching–and yes, laughing–exercises.

Her bank is a recent convert to one of the latest worker-motivation activities: laughter therapy. Research has proven that laughter relieves stress, reduces anxiety and increases mental energy. Laughter therapy is designed to keep workers in a good mood so that they'll be friendlier to customers.

Does it work? Well, everybody has a good time trying it out. Whether or not we need a club, laughter is good for you and those around you.

My heart is glad, and my soul rejoices. (Psalm 16:9)

Fill me with joy, Father–and help me radiate that joy to others.

A Taxing Question

Ever heard of someone wanting to pay more, rather than less, taxes? Meet Charles Demere and Michele McGeoy. According to *Hope* magazine they are part of Responsible Wealth, "a national group whose 400 prosperous members say wealthy Americans ought to shoulder more of the nation's tax burden."

Members of Responsible Wealth reject capital gains tax breaks and donate millions to "nonprofit organizations working to narrow the gap between rich and poor." They advocate bringing the salaries of CEO and hourly/salaried employees more in line with each other.

McGeoy says she is more interested in building a healthy society than in building her personal wealth.

What can you do to build a healthy and just society?

A person is justified by works and not by faith... As the body without the spirit is dead, so faith without works is also dead. (James 2:24,26)

Show me, Lord, ways to make a difference for those struggling with poverty.

The Path to Charity

Moses Maimonides, a Spanish-born Jewish philosopher, greatly influenced Christian thought in the Middle Ages through his treatise, *The Guide for the Perplexed*. Here are his insightful eight steps to charity, from the least to the most virtuous.

- First...to give with reluctance or regret.
- Second, give cheerfully but not proportionately to the distress of the sufferer.
- Third, to give cheerfully and proportionately, but not until asked.
- Fourth, to give unsolicited.
- Fifth, sixth and seventh, to give bountifully, enthusiastically and anonymously.
- Eighth and most meritorious, to prevent poverty–by assisting those in need with a gift or a loan to get them on their feet, or teaching them how to earn a decent living, even to opening one's own home to them.

Look for opportunities to do charity in your immediate family, in your community and in the wider world.

The measure you give will be the measure you get back. (Luke 6:38)

May I seek ways to give to those in need, Generous Giver.

"Have Courage and Joy"

Writer Madeleine L'Engle had three books published before she was thirty. Then she had some tough years, getting more than two dozen rejections before a publisher accepted *A Wrinkle in Time*. The 1962 book won the American Library Association's Newbery Medal for children's literature. It also won the hearts of millions of young readers.

The author produced another two dozen books, as well as a "philosophy of failure": "If I'm not free to fail, I'm not free to take risks, and everything in life that's worth doing involves a willingness to risk failure. ...The same is true in all human relationships. Unless I'm willing to open myself up to risk and to being hurt, then, I'm closing myself to love and friendship." She adds, "Sometimes our moments of greatest joy come at times of greatest courage."

Make room for risk and courage in your life and you will find joy as well.

Deal courageously. (2 Chronicles 19:11)

Holy Spirit, grant me the bravery to face failure, risk and change. Remind me that You are always here for me.

Meaningful Penance

June Leman couldn't forgive herself for an incident in her life. She sought a spiritual counselor's advice. "God forgave you before you even thought about it," he said. "You need to forgive yourself." He suggested that penance might make it easier.

Leman spoke to the head of a local soup kitchen. She saw herself ladling stew to the grateful homeless and becoming their confidante. Instead, she was asked to take charge of the laundry.

Ironically, Leman hated doing laundry. But as odious as the job was, she began to care about all the aprons, washcloths and towels she washed, dried and folded. She found her work rewarding and two years later was asked to become the clerk for their board of directors–even though she hated note taking!

Doing penance can help us become better people, if we realize that we need to forgive ourselves as much as others.

We do not have a high priest who is unable to sympathize with our weaknesses, but...one who in every respect has been tested as we are, yet without sin. (Hebrews 4:15)

Merciful Savior, free us from inhuman perfectionism which makes us unable to forgive ourselves.

Dashing through Life

What's the measure of a life? This excerpt from an anonymous poem that appeared in *Bits & Pieces* offers a new slant.

I read of a man who stood up to speak
At the funeral of a friend.
He referred to the dates on her tombstone
From the beginning to the end.
He noted that first came the date of birth
And spoke the following date with tears.
But said what mattered most of all
Was the dash between the years.
For that dash represents all the time
That she had spent alive on earth.
And now only those who loved her know
What that little line is worth...

We don't choose our birth date or death date, but we do decide how we live the in-between. Make the most of your life.

Remember your Creator in the days of your youth. (Ecclesiastes 12:1)

Trinity, time is so short; eternity so long. Teach me to put my life and Your love in perspective.

Many Questions, One Answer

Family and work, household tasks and social obligations absorb our attention. Yet, few of us do not, at some time, ponder creation and our place in the universe.

St. Gregory Nazianzen, a bishop, did so in the 4th century. He wrote: "Recognize to Whom you owe the fact that you exist, that you breathe, that you understand...

"What benefactor has enabled you to look upon the beauty of the sky, the sun in its course, the circle of the moon, the countless stars, with the harmony and order that is theirs? Who has blessed you with...food, with the arts and education, with houses, with laws, with a life of humanity and culture, with friendship and the easy familiarity of kinship?

"It is God, then Who asks you now, in your turn, to show yourself generous."

We can never match God's bounty. But we can offer Him our thanks and ourselves.

Give thanks to the Lord...who...made the heavens...spread out the earth...made the great lights, for His steadfast love endures forever. (Psalm 136: 3,5,6,7)

Thank You, God of grace and graciousness. Teach me to mirror Your generosity.

The Mysterious, Glorious Condor

The California condor is one of the largest and rarest birds on earth. But why the condor survived into the 20th century while other species became extinct is a mystery.

The majestic condor once shared North America with wooly mammoths and saber-toothed tigers. And the condor was showing signs of decline some 20,000 years ago, most likely due to the arrival of humans in North America.

By the end of the 19th century, the range of the great bird had narrowed to the mountains of California and parts of Mexico. More recently, the danger of extinction increased due to overpopulation, development and pesticides.

Today, there are approximately 160 California Condors. While most are in captivity, others are slowly being reintroduced to the wild. And thanks to the tireless efforts of those dedicated to wildlife preservation, their numbers continue to increase.

Share your respect for all creation with those around you.

God said, "...let birds fly above the earth across the dome of the sky." (Genesis 1:20)

God, bless those who care enough about Your earth to help preserve its beauty, its creatures.

A Choice Attitude

"When I made the decision to stop being miserable, I didn't know how I'd feel," says Joanne Kuttner. "I still have moments of self-doubt, but that decision changed my life."

Kuttner battled shyness and a lack of self-esteem until she was in her mid-twenties. When she consciously changed her attitude, her career took a new direction, she met new friends, married and started a family.

Fortunately, most of us only have to fight against bad moods on an occasional basis. Dr. David Myers, author of *The Pursuit of Happiness*, has two recommendations for people interested in boosting their happiness quotients: "Do little things day-to-day that can change your mood, and, over a lifetime, adopt the activities of happy people. ...It's nearly impossible to stay in a dark mood when you're listening to upbeat music."

You can choose your attitude. Choose a happy one!

David and all...Israel were dancing before the Lord with songs, and lyres and harps and tambourines and castanets and cymbals.
(2 Samuel 6:5)

Give me the energy and will, Spirit of Life, to improve my outlook.

Wall Dogs?

"Wall dogs" are a dying breed but in their heyday these sign painters helped advertise everything from Coca-Cola to the local "carriage manufactory" with skill and flair.

"A hand-painted sign by a good artist has nuances that a printed sign does not have," according to one of the few remaining wall dogs.

The handiwork of these skilled advertising sign painters from the early 1900s is still evident today, especially in places such as New York City. Artisans whose canvases were the brick walls of buildings, "combined the lettering ability of scribes with the stamina of mountain climbers and the agility and daring of circus acrobats," writes Linda Cooper Bowen in *Preservation*.

Over the decades, the colors in the hand-painted signs have often faded but the letters remain visible. They tell of another era when rooms rented "from $2.50" or you could "Dial Joe 1234" for information about his business.

Look around you, not only for the present, but the past.

The memory of the righteous is a blessing, but the name of the wicked will rot. (Proverbs 10:7)

Guide my hand, Lord, as I paint on Your canvas which is my life.

Can You See What I See?

Seventeen-year-old Tim Gethers had to complete fifteen hours of community service in order to graduate from his high school. He was not looking forward to the requirement, but agreed to refurbish an old mailbox at the suggestion of the school's community service coordinator.

The mailbox was to be one of several which would be placed around town so that people could drop off their used prescription glasses. Fifteen hours into the project, Tim was only half finished. He not only followed through until it was complete, but also agreed to refurbish a second mailbox.

Classmates have since collected and measured the prescription strength of hundreds of eyeglasses which will be distributed by a team of optometrists on a mission trip to Mexico.

"Helping other people, it's a good gesture," says Tim. "To tell you the truth, it makes me feel good."

Do good—you'll feel good, too.

**Those who are generous are blessed.
(Proverbs 22:9)**

Remind us, Heavenly Father, of how deeply we are rewarded when we reach out to others.

TV Can be Hazardous to Your Time

In most American homes, children and parents turn on the television after school or work.

Such a simple, seemingly harmless act can have unintended consequences. On average, U.S. youngsters see 360,000 commercials and witness 200,000 acts of violence, including 16,000 murders, by the time they're 18 years of age.

How much do you depend on television daily? Would you have additional time to spend with friends and family if the television were turned off? Has television alienated you from others?

The more time you spend watching TV, the less you have for your family. In this busy world, it doesn't make sense to waste hour after hour watching stories of other people's lives rather than enjoying your own.

Time is precious. Strike a balance. Be sure to keep your family in its rightful place.

We do not live to ourselves, and we do not die to ourselves. (Romans 14:7)

I cannot live without the companionship of loved ones, Triune God. Bless them. Bless me.

Age Is Just a Number

Are you feeling a little older today, a bit blue about the encroaching years on the personal calendar? If you're thinking it's too late for you to make your mark, think again. Take a look at some of these inspiring examples of "older" achievers:

- Michelangelo was 71 when he painted the Sistine Chapel.

- George Burns won his first Oscar at age 80.

- Grandma Moses didn't start painting until she was 80; 25 percent of her paintings were produced when she was past 100.

- Casey Stengel managed the New York Mets until he was 75.

- Doc Counsilman was 58 when he became the oldest person to swim the English Channel.

Don't give up because of age. You're never too old to try and to succeed.

Do not be too righteous, and do not act too wise; why should you destroy yourself? Do not be too wicked, and do not be a fool; why should you die before your time? (Ecclesiastes 7:16-17)

Help me face the years with optimism and joy, Jesus.

Precursor to the Pyramids?

It's been said that success is ten percent inspiration and ninety percent perspiration. Still, without an idea or a vision, many wonders of the world might not exist.

Consider the great pyramids of Egypt's Giza Plateau. Commissioned more than 4,600 years ago by pharaohs of the fourth dynasty, they are the oldest of the seven wonders of the ancient world and the only ones still standing.

While it's no secret that constructing these great creations entailed the backbreaking work of thousands, what inspired the project? One writer thinks their design was inspired by the natural landforms of the eastern Sahara Desert. Many of these huge forms resemble the general shape of the pyramids.

Inspiration is a funny thing. It cannot be forced and, often, it comes to us at the most unexpected times and in the most unlikely of places. We just have to stay open to it.

Give ear, O My people, to My teaching; incline your ears to the words of My mouth. (Psalm 78:1)

Holy Spirit, inspire me to be a better person, especially when it is most challenging.

Think Before You Speak

The University of Washington is home to important new research into communication between spouses. "We see the responses of spouses to both destructive and helpful fight behaviors," says psychologist Sybil Carrere.

Here are phrases from Carrere's book, *Love to Last a Lifetime*, to make disputes more productive:

- "It's important to me to know what you're thinking."
- "What can we both do to make this situation better?"–your relationship is the priority.
- "I was upset when you corrected me in front of your parents" shows anger without degradation.
- "I'm sorry I hurt you" means not being bogged down by who was right or wrong.

When disagreeing with a spouse or a friend do so with an eye to improving your relationship, not harming it.

Those with good sense are slow to anger, and it is their glory to overlook an offense. (Proverbs 19:11)

Lord, enable me to treat my loved ones with the respect they deserve.

Lights, Camera, Action!

Think California and images of screen stars and movie premieres come to mind. Dorothy Thompson was enjoying a successful career producing commercials when, on April 29,1992, she saw Los Angeles' streets full of angry rioters.

Watching the lootings and beatings in horror, she realized that she did not know a single African-American or Latino who worked in production. She decided to train people of diverse ethnic backgrounds in her business.

Ms. Thompson's non-profit *Streetlights Program* takes determined people and puts them through a free intensive training program. They are prepared for entry-level positions as production assistants.

Success stories abound. *Streetlights* graduates work for every major Hollywood film studio. An East L.A. woman put it succinctly: "The bulb was there; *Streetlights* just turned on the power. Dorothy (Thompson) wants us all to shine."

Strike a spark of hope for someone today.

She...reaches out her hands to the needy. (Proverbs 31:20)

Open our eyes to possibilities, Holy One.

More than Baseball

To baseball fans, Derek Jeter is an accomplished major leaguer. To his parents and those he helps in his spare time, he's a caring young man.

Jeter knows that his very presence can bring a smile to the faces of hospitalized children during his visits. That's why he makes a effort to help youngsters.

"When Derek does something like this, I'm as proud of him as when he does something in baseball," said Dr. Charles Jeter, executive director of his son's charitable organization, "Turn 2 Foundation."

The younger Jeter developed his feeling of responsibility to care for others from his parents. He also realizes that "people look up to you if you play for the Yankees. I think you should do something to help out."

We all have responsibilities to care about and for others.

Do to others as you would have them do to you. (Luke 6:31)

Inspire us to lives of whole-souled generosity, Jesus.

One Beautiful Life

Growing up in poverty in St. Mary's County in Maryland, Thomas Forbes never went to school because his family needed him on the farm. As he grew, Forbes would work in several trades—plumbing, bricklaying, cement finishing; he even dug graves.

But one thing that Forbes didn't do, until he was nearly 60, was learn to read. His incentive: "I heard a call from God telling me to do more for His people," he said. He decided to become a permanent deacon in the Roman Catholic Church. His wife and a retired teacher helped him.

Forbes loved serving as a deacon, ministering to the sick and shut-ins, taking part in funerals, weddings, baptisms and marriage preparation classes. Before his death at age 75, he said, "I'm happy the Lord has led me this way, so I can reach out to people. I have a beautiful life."

He did, indeed.

Deacons likewise must be serious; ...they must hold fast to...the faith with a clear conscience. (1 Timothy 3:8,9)

From the rising to the setting of the sun, You guide me, Lord, giving me strength in all my work for You.

A Time to Be Reborn

It's almost hard not to celebrate once spring rolls around, but here are some ideas for enjoying the simple pleasures of the season by yourself or with loved ones:

- Open every window and breathe in the fresh air.
- Go for a walk, even in the rain, and pay attention to the scents around you.
- Pick a bouquet. Give it to someone who can't get out.
- Stand under a dogwood, magnolia or apple tree when the petals are falling.
- Resolve to be happy.

This last idea may be a challenge, but spring is a good time to remember that God's earth is bursting with blessings. Seek them out. Be grateful.

The earth will be full of the knowledge of the Lord as the waters cover the sea. (Isaiah 11:9)

Thank you, Generous Creator, for the freshness of each season.

Honest Talk about Cheating

According to recent studies, teens are surrendering to the temptation to cheat more and more often. One survey of students at 31 schools found that 70 percent of the young people admitted to cheating at some point during college; 15 percent saw themselves as "serious, repetitive cheaters."

Cheating in school, says Thomas Lickona, author of *Educating for Character*, can lead to cheating in other situations in life: in dating relationships, on after-school jobs, in sports.

One student, Jillian, copied her friend's homework and surfed the net for term papers and essay assignments; gave price breaks to friends at her after-school grocery store job and lied to her boyfriend so she could date another. It was only after Jillian was fired that she recognized the pattern of dishonesty. She took a long, hard look at her behavior and made changes for the better.

Look carefully at your life and your level of integrity.

One who gives an honest answer gives a kiss on the lips. (Proverbs 24:26)

You are the source of truth and goodness, Father, lead me in Your way this day.

Your Children As Friends

When our children reach adulthood, it's time to relate to them as adults. Clinical social worker Ralph Ranieri offers a few tips for the older generation to avoid strained relationships with "the people closest to us."

Appreciate adult children as the people they actually are. "Appreciating them means accepting them with all their warts, mistakes, problems and baggage."

Remember our children aren't here for our fulfillment. Their main goal isn't to please us but "to do what they think is God's will for them."

Don't hold grudges. Forgive old hurts and start today to enjoy whatever time you have together. You never know how much time you will have.

Respect by each generation for the other will go a long way toward developing a rewarding relationship, adult to adult.

Whoever does not receive the kingdom of God as a little child will never enter it. (Luke 18:17)

Bless us, Lord, in our efforts to reevaluate and improve our relationships.

Sultan of Smooth

Joe DiMaggio, Mickey Mantle, Reggie Jackson, Derek Jeter, each of these, plus many other baseball players and countless fans have heard the mellifluous voice of Bob Sheppard. Since 1951, he has been "the Voice of the New York Yankees."

After serving in the Navy during World War II, the announcer taught speech to high school students. He has also announced for the NFL's New York Giants since the mid-fifties.

Sheppard's favorite sports moment? Don Larsen's perfect game against the Dodgers in the 1956 World Series. His "rules for public address?" "Be clear, concise, correct. Never cute or comic or corny."

The voice can be a powerful tool to foster anger and despair or hopefulness and joy. The choice is yours.

The words of the wicked are a deadly ambush, but the speech of the upright delivers them. (Proverbs 12:6)

Fill me, Holy Spirit, with a desire to bring the best that is in me to all I do.

Making the Impossible Possible

At the end of the 19th century, a 17-year-old climbed a tree to trim some branches and, as he wrote in his diary, "was a different boy when I descended from when I ascended, for existence at last seemed purposive."

That young man was Robert Goddard, a founding father of the space age, and the purpose to which he committed himself was the idea of space flight.

In 1926, the first flight of a liquid-fuel rocket was achieved by Goddard: launched from his aunt's cabbage patch. His early achievements set the stage for the beginning of the space age, yet he always struggled to find support for his experiments. He once said to a reporter: "Every vision is a joke until the first man accomplishes it; once realized, it becomes commonplace."

Regardless of the wonders of our technological age, we should never grow so jaded that a visionary's view of the future becomes a commonplace event.

There is hope for your future, says the Lord. (Jeremiah 31:17)

Only You know what is impossible for us, Creator.

As Simple as You Want it to Be

When writer Anne Lamott's son, Sam, was offered a complimentary paragliding ride for his birthday, she thought she'd collapse from fright.

After her initial shock, "What confused me was how much freedom I was supposed to give Sam," says Lamott. Unclear about the line between good parenting and being overly protective, she prayed a favorite prayer: "Help me. Help me."

In meditation, Lamott reached a decision. Later, in the shadow of the mountain Sam would not be jumping off, they asked God to help them come up with "a really exciting and safe way for Sam to celebrate his birthday." He and friends enjoyed inner-tubing on a nearby creek. And Lamott was happy to say another favorite prayer: "Thank You! Thank You!"

Our interaction with God can be simple or complex. The choice is ours.

Trust in the Lord with all your heart and...He will make straight your paths. (Proverbs 3:5,6)

Enable parents to commit their fears, hopes and joys to You, Jesus, who described Yourself as a hen trying to gather her chicks under her wings.

A Fitness Fix for Your Cupboard

What are the must-have items for every kitchen pantry? Nutrition writer Jean Carper offers a list of 22 cupboard staples.

An advisor on food and medicine, she says we should stock up on: roasted red peppers in jars; frozen spinach; onions; blueberries; apples; oranges or orange juice; salmon or sardines, fresh or canned; ground turkey breast; canned chickpeas; canned tomatoes; brown rice: whole-wheat bread ("whole wheat should be the first ingredient listed"); oats; tea, black or green; walnuts; prunes; extra virgin olive oil; balsamic vinegar; fresh garlic; and multivitamins.

Many of these items work well in casseroles, stews, stir-fries or soups. Stock up on them, says Carper, and "you'll always have the right ingredients on hand to eat smart."

So take inventory—and get shopping for healthier days!

The dead will be raised imperishable...For this perishable body must put on imperishability, and this mortal body...immortality.
(1 Corinthians 15:52,53)

Nourish me, Father, with Your Word; refresh my soul when I grow weary.

Antwone's Lesson

Antwone Fisher's father, Edward Elkins, died before he was born. Afterwards, his mother abandoned him. Growing up in the foster care system, Antwone knew only abuse and despair.

Yet he chose to make a decent life for himself. After service in the Navy, Antwone became a security guard in Los Angeles. On the side, he diligently worked the phone until he connected with his father's sister in Cleveland.

His new family members located his mother within a few months. Standing outside her apartment, Antwone rehearsed the speech he'd prepared for 33 years.

The moment the door opened, anger and confusion melted into compassion. Antwone embraced the frail, tiny woman before him. She turned away in shame, leaving the room in tears.

"Though my road had been long and hard," Antwone wrote, "I finally understood that my mother's had been longer and harder."

A wise child makes a glad father, but the foolish despise their mothers. (Proverbs 15:20)

Fill us with tenderness, Merciful God.

Desserts Change a Community

Property values are rising and crime is down in the area around Amadou Diakite's Sweet Chef Southern Style Bakery in Harlem. New businesses are moving in to improve the area. Customers are bringing their dollars to the local economy. What started this much needed relief for the area? Mr. Diakite's pies.

He started out selling his sweet potato, navy bean, apple crumb and other pies to markets and restaurants. When neighbors smelled them baking, they urged him to make them available. He added a retail shop and the results have gone beyond his wildest dreams. The baker's success has created jobs and improved a neighborhood.

We never know which of our efforts, however small, will better the world around us. All we can do is keep trying.

The good person brings good things out of a good treasure. (Matthew 12:35)

Inspire me, Lord, and make me generous with that inspiration.

Bear-ly There

When Susan Cheever had a baby, it seemed everyone sent her a stuffed animal. But only Snuffles the bear caught the little one's fancy.

Like parents the world over, Cheever watched as her daughter loved the fur right off Snuffles. The baby thought the teddy bear was a cat and named it "Meow" or "Me" for short.

After a while, Susan Cheever began to worry about Me's survival. She even dreamed about the toy, so central to her daughter's happiness. When her daughter was three, she saw an identical bear for sale. She was smart enough to know Me could never be replaced. But that night, she sneaked into her daughter's room to do a little replacement surgery on one leg.

It worked. Bit by bit, Susan Cheever replaced parts as necessary. "Too much love can destroy," she mused, "but it can also repair and mend."

Love is patient...kind...not envious or boastful or arrogant or rude. ...not irritable or resentful. (1 Corinthians 13:4,5)

Bit by bit, Lord, repair our hurts. Help us tend others, too.

The Keeper of the Light

When Frank Schubert took a job with the U.S. Lighthouse Service in 1937, he didn't know that it would become his life-long passion or that he would become the last civilian lighthouse-keeper in the country.

Now in his eighties, Schubert has been the keeper of Coney Island Light Station for more than 40 years. His job almost ended in 1989 when the lighthouse was automated. But the Coast Guard decided to keep him on duty. Schubert, who once climbed a narrow, winding 87-step staircase to the light room, where he tended the light by cranking a grandfather-clock mechanism that rotated its beacon, still raises the American and Coast Guard flags and maintains the grounds.

Schubert learned to counter the isolation of lighthouse-keeping with hobbies like marquetry or golf. Occasionally, he'll give a tour to visitors. "It is," Schubert says, "a good life."

Whatever you do, your life can be good, if you make it so.

Live...in a manner worthy of the gospel of Christ. (Philippians 1:27)

You are the true Light, Lord. Show us Your way.

More Than Meets the Eye

Nowadays, people may think of George Foreman as the guy who sells hamburger grills or who promotes car muffler services in television commercials.

What some may not know or have forgotten, is that the popular pitchman won an Olympic gold medal for boxing in 1968, and heavyweight titles in 1973 and again in 1994 at age 45. More than that, he is an ordained minister and a writer, runs a youth center in Houston, Texas, and is the father of ten children – including five sons named George.

People are hardly one-dimensional. Yet, we often judge others based on what we see on the surface. Learn to look inside.

Why do you...say to your neighbor, 'Let me take the speck out of your eye,' while the log is in your own eye? (Matthew 7:3,4)

Lord, remind me that appearances are usually misleading.

Getting a Life

In a commencement address delivered at Villanova University in Pennsylvania, newspaper columnist Anna Quindlen had this advice for graduates.

"Get a life. A real life, not a manic pursuit of the next promotion, the bigger paycheck, the larger house.

"Get a life in which you notice the smell of salt water pushing itself on a breeze. Get a life in which you stop and watch how a red-tailed hawk circles over the water gap, or the way a baby scowls with concentration when she tries to pick up a Cheerio with her thumb and first finger.

"Get a life in which you are not alone. Find people you love, and who love you. And remember that love is not leisure; it is work. Each time you look at your diploma, remember that you are still a student, still learning how to best treasure your connection to others."

People matter. Love matters. Life matters.

(Love) bears...believes...hopes...endures all things... never ends. (1 Corinthians 13:7,8)

This day, help me, Creator, to bring Your life and love to those in need.

Do You Worry too Much?

Everyone worries occasionally, but for some anxiety is so pervasive that it rules and ruins their lives.

Therapist Reid Wilson, author of *Don't Panic: Taking Control of Anxiety Attacks,* believes some people "worry at the wrong times, for the wrong reasons and for too long."

He notes, "people with anxiety disorders act as though worry were an intimate friend and protector rather than an annoying and only occasionally helpful acquaintance." They are also "inappropriately wedded to certainty; don't want any surprises (and) forget that mistakes have always been an essential part of learning...taking risks, part of being alive."

Dr. Wilson thinks that the anxiety-plagued must face their fears so their "innate courage" can bloom.

Truth-be-told, many of us are anxious about something; want no surprises in some areas of life. That's limiting.

Ask yourself how you can face your fears and allow your "innate courage" to bloom.

Be strong and courageous. (Joshua 1:6)

May I pursue Your will with courage and passion, Holy Spirit.

A Little Texas in Times Square?

It's hard to imagine, but New York may be just the place to get a taste of Texas.

At least that's what admirers of singer Jerry Jeff Walker say, when he plays to New York audiences. Some say it's as if the Lone Star State was "infused into the Big Apple." But while he considers himself a Texan, the fact is, he was born in New York's Catskill Mountains.

Still, it's not only Walker's down-home sound that keeps fans loyal. "His singing is gentle and introspective," says one fan. Others say his willingness to "dig into quiet emotions is what draws fans from Texas and elsewhere."

What do you find attractive in others? What do others say they find attractive in you? These are first steps on the royal road to self-knowledge.

Revere the Lord, and serve Him in sincerity and in faithfulness. (Joshua 24:14)

Jesus, You are the truth and the way. I pray I can emulate You and remain truthful and sincere in my dealings with myself and with others.

Spouses Keeping Secrets

A Reader's Digest poll of 1,000 people showed that about 40 percent of American spouses keep secrets from one another.

Apparently, it's mostly about finances. Close to half said they kept quiet about what they really paid for an item.

"You always get those 'good bargains,' you know," said one woman. Said another, "I don't like to tell him how much I spend when I go shopping."

Other areas of secrecy include failure at work and a child's behavior. One parent said that sometimes the kids behave in ways that would make their spouse go "ballistic" if they knew. And 20 percent said they had dreams they haven't mentioned to a spouse.

What reasons do people give for the secrecy? Guilt motivates some; others, the desire to avoid hurting a partner's feelings.

Whatever the reasons given, married couples need to keep talking–honestly–with each other.

Birds roost with their own kind, so honesty comes home to those who practice it. (Sirach 27:9)

Dear God, show us Your way.

Harmony in Helping

Grammy Award-winning producer, arranger and composer Quincy Jones feels fortunate to have found music at a young age. "Music grabbed me around the throat and has been there ever since," he says. "I was blessed."

Wanting to help children who have not found harmony in their lives, Jones started the Quincy Jones Listen Up Foundation to "confront the state of emergency that threatens the world's youth." The foundation's projects help give young people a new perspective on life, while aiming to match Jones's high-powered show business associations with community organizations that need more attention and resources.

Any way in which Jones can help children is fine by him. "It's a ray of hope when they realize they can expect more from their lives," he says.

Think about casting a "ray of hope" for the younger people in your community. Reach out today in your own unique way.

Sow for yourselves righteousness. (Hosea 10:12)

Your example inspires me to harmonize with others, Lord.

The Frugal Donor

Mary Hutto was so thrifty that she used to sleep in the hallway of her boardinghouse so that a tenant could use each room.

This frugality, along with a shrewd investing sense, enabled Hutto to amass a fortune worth $3.5 million. Upon her death at 95, she donated it to her alma mater, Western Kentucky University, which was near her home. Her bequest will allow 70 students to receive $2500 annual scholarships.

A giving spirit lives on after the person is gone. Think about the legacy you want to leave behind.

The good leave an inheritance to their children's children. (Proverbs 13:22)

May I never forget to give what I can, generous One. May I never cease to be grateful for all that I receive from Your hands and from Your children.

Hooked on Plastic

"Just charge it" has become a national mantra, encouraged by a credit card industry that aggressively courts us.

If you worry about debt, if you use credit cards to pay for routine expenses, and if you make only minimum payments on your cards, you could have a "plastic problem."

Here are a few tips for managing debt:

- Pay off high-rate debt first and eliminate your most expensive debt.
- Think about consolidating your debt into a lower rate loan.
- Negotiate with lenders, showing them you intend to pay your bills.
- Get help by consulting a non-profit credit counseling service.

Take responsibility for using your money and all your resources well.

The protection of wisdom is like the protection of money. (Ecclesiastes 7:12)

Spirit, give me Your guidance in managing money.

"Don't Mess with Seniors"

Officials of Evergreen Plaza, a suburban Chicago, Illinois, shopping mall, created a controversy when they tried to bar senior "mall walkers." These legions of sneaker-clad, often elderly, walkers begin their day by exercising in climate-controlled shopping spaces. The mall served notice that it would no longer be available to walkers.

Amidst a barrage of bad publicity, boycott threats and patron poaching from nearby malls, Evergreen officials were forced to relent. Said one member of the Council of Shopping Centers, "Mall walking is pretty much a given and something that is hard for malls to avoid."

Bob Strickland, president of the Mall Walkers Steering Committee, counsels forgiveness of those who would try to ban mall walkers. He says, "you don't want to mess with seniors."

Whatever your age, if some cause matters to you, be willing to get active and involved.

Rise before the aged, and defer to the old. (Leviticus 19:32)

Lord Jesus, grant me good health and a positive outlook.

Seeing Green

What do Central Park, the Museum of Natural History, the Metropolitan Museum of Art, the Bronx Zoo, Riverside Park and the New York Public Library have in common?

In three words: Andrew Haswell Green.

Born in 1820 in Massachusetts, Green moved to New York as a teenager, and later became a lawyer. In 1857, Green stepped up to head the commission to design and build Central Park, presiding over all park work for the next 13 years. In fact, in his lifetime, he planned, improved and beautified the city, creating and building homes for many of New York's greatest cultural institutions. Green also pushed for the consolidation of the five boroughs that now make up New York City.

Only a granite bench in Central Park remains in his memory. Yet whether they know it or not, all who sit there do see Green in the beauty he left behind.

May all we do honor God and benefit His people.

**Remember the deeds of the ancestors.
(1 Maccabees 2:51)**

The gifts You give us, Master, may they glorify You.

Recreating Her World

A rare autoimmune disease had left 50-year-old Lisa Fittipaldi blind and depressed. When her husband, Al, learned that art might be good therapy for her, he bought watercolors and challenged her to "just do something." Fittipaldi, who had never drawn before, presented him with a picture of four jars.

Today, Lisa Fittipaldi's watercolors and oils hang in more than 30 galleries nationwide. Says one of her former art instructors, "she captures the true inner spirit more than most sighted artists. She paints from the heart."

Refusing to dwell on her blindness, Fittipaldi also studies yoga and cooks and bakes for guests at the bed and breakfast she and Al opened last year.

But mostly she credits art with saving her life. "When you lose your vision, you lose your world. My painting recreated my world."

Enjoy the senses that God gave you.

God saw everything that He had made...was very good. (Genesis 1:31)

Thank You for the vision to see beauty in Your world, Jesus.

How Much Do You Really Know?

One Internet wag isn't so sure you know it all and came up with a list of unusual items. Here are a few of the oddities that the e-mailer says are facts:

- Rubber bands last longer when refrigerated.
- Peanuts are an ingredient in dynamite.
- There are 293 ways to make change for a dollar.
- A shark is the only fish that can blink with both eyes.
- Two-thirds of the world's eggplant is grown in New Jersey.
- The longest one syllable word in English is screeched.
- All 50 states are on the top of the Lincoln Memorial on the back of the $5 bill.
- Maine is the only state whose name is just one syllable.

Unfortunately, genuine wisdom doesn't come from just knowing facts. Good judgment and prudence to use knowledge well, are even more vital.

Wisdom is from the Lord, and...was created before all other things. (Sirach 1:1,4)

Holy Spirit, grant us wisdom.

Learning How to Live Again

"Slowly regaining consciousness, the altered vision my eyes conveyed felt more like a dream than reality. I was experiencing life for the first time, seeing the world through infant eyes. ...Confined to the bed, I closed my eyes, silent, completely detached from the dilemma that was now my life."

Writing in *TBI Challenge* about the traumatic brain injury she'd sustained in a car accident nine years earlier, the woman conveyed the many frustrations of a long recovery.

She had to relearn speech: it's easy to take it for granted until you realize what's involved. Overcoming depression was another challenge.

"It has taken a lot of conscious effort, perseverance and determination to get me where I am today, but the void has been replaced with a passion for life....Things in life happen for a reason and it's up to us to realize our purpose."

Seek God's will in understanding your purpose here.

The Lord is my shepherd. (Psalm 23:1)

Help us, Good Shepherd, to follow You moment by moment.

Of Medals and Memories

If Memorial Day has become just another reason to take off work and have a picnic, take a moment to consider the Congressional Medal of Honor. Our nation's highest recognition for valor in combat, only 3,410 people have received it since 1862.

Brian Thacker received the medal after he called in artillery strikes on himself while being overrun by the enemy in Kontum Province, Vietnam. Harvey Barnum, Jr., led his men, outnumbered 12 to 1, out of an ambush to safety .

The about 150 living recipients of the medal have an annual meeting. One recipient, James Allen Taylor, says "our personal lives and beliefs have a common thread that bonds us together: unwavering love and devotion to our country."

Do you value the rights and privileges of your country?

He heard of the battles that Jonathan and his brothers had fought, of the brave deeds...and of the troubles. (1 Maccabees 10:15)

Strengthen our determination to preserve the freedoms and responsibilities guaranteed by the Constitution and Bill of Rights, Author of our Liberties.

Word Pictures

"Rolle bolle."

This seemingly nonsensical phrase is actually part of a *Dictionary of American Regional English,* which was edited by Frederic G. Cassidy. He followed his love of folk language into the nooks and crannies of the Creole language of his native Jamaica and across the linguistic expanses of the United States. He died in 2000 at the age of 92.

In putting together the dictionary, this English professor sent researchers into the countryside with tape recorders and a list of 1,847 questions about what people call things.

"My father loved words from the moment he was a very small child," his daughter, Claire, says.

By the way, rolle bolle is a game with similarities to bowling and horseshoes common in Dutch and Belgian settlement areas. And, the next time you get irritated, just say "piffleberries."

Are not all these who are speaking Galileans? And how is it that we hear, each of us, in our own native language? (Acts 2:7-8)

Help me to find You, Lord, in the details of this day.

In the Eyes of Children

Photographer Wendy Ewald believes children have a unique way of looking at things and stories that only they can tell.

"People's conceptions of children are very far from who children actually are," Ms. Ewald said. "Because they don't speak for themselves, there are so many stereotypes."

Ms. Ewald has taught children ages 10 to 13 worldwide how to use the tools of her trade so they can document their experiences using photos, writings and recordings.

Youngsters don't sugarcoat their experiences and often describe their fears as they face brutal realities. A girl from the Indian subcontinent described the troubles young brides have and how she'd rather die than have to get married.

In Kentucky "there was a sense of preserving what was old...the greater home of the mountains, and traditions...like the boys going raccoon hunting, or making molasses."

Ask a child to share his or her story.

Whoever welcomes one such child in My name welcomes Me, and...the One who sent Me. (Mark 9:37)

Lord of Life, help adults truly hear children.

A Word with God

An anonymous author imagined an interview in which the questioner asked God what most amazed Him about humankind. God was amazed at how many people:

- lose their health to make money and then lose their money to restore their health;
- by being anxious about the future forget the present, living neither for the present nor the future.

And what guidance would God give on life's important lessons? God asked men and women to learn that:

- what is most valuable is not what but who they have in their lives;
- it is not good to compare themselves to others;
- practicing forgiveness is the way to learn to forgive;
- two people see the same thing differently.

God is our always-available, ever-loving Father.

I know My own and My own know Me, just as the Father knows Me and I know the Father. (John 10:14-15)

Help me ask for advice as needed, Abba.

A Spouse's Support + Motivation

Doris Abreu is trying to take care of her health by staying fit. Like most of us, she has found there are some mornings when her regimen seems impossible. She found a solution for those "why bother" days: her husband, Fidel.

The Abreus attend an early morning exercise class each week and greet every Sunday with a three or four-mile walk.

"There are times when the alarm goes off at 5:00 a.m. and you're like, 'Oh, no'," Doris explains. It's on those mornings that she is most grateful for the team approach to fitness. When one wants to give up, "the other one (says) 'Let's go! Let's go!'" she adds.

There is no burden, great or small, that cannot be lessened by sharing it with loved ones. We are here together. Let us be here for each other.

Bear one another's burdens, and...fulfill the law of Christ. (Galatians 6:2)

Make me strong enough for others to lean on and strong enough to lean on others, Holy Spirit.

Who Am I?

Here is a patriotic puzzle from cyberspace that you will probably solve very easily.

I stand watch in America's halls of justice.

I am recognized all over the world.

I am revered and I am saluted.

I have fought in every battle of every war for more than 200 years.

I was battle-worn and tired, but soldiers cheered me.

I have stood watch over the uncharted frontiers of space from my vantage point on the moon.

When I lie in the trembling arms of a grieving parent at the grave of their fallen son or daughter, I am proud.

My name is *Old Glory,* the flag of the United States.

Take your civic responsibilities seriously.

Lord, You are my Father; do not forsake me in the days of trouble. (Sirach 51:10)

Father, inspire us to live the values represented by our nation's stars and stripes.

God the Career Counselor

Sara Holtz graduated from high school with honors and a detailed plan for her future. She earned her bachelor's degree from the College of William and Mary and went to work for a multinational, Fortune 500 company. Holtz was a "success."

None of those accomplishments, however, are the reason her former high school in Rolling Meadows, Illinois, presented her with an alumni award. Instead, it was because she volunteered for three years with the Peace Corps' Safer Motherhood and Childhood Survival Project. Holz taught West Africans about nutrition, hygiene and disease prevention.

"I love working directly with these peasant farmers to improve their health and daily lives," says Holtz.

She went on to study for her masters of public health and returned to Africa to do AIDS research.

"Success" has many meanings. It's never too late to aim for the success that really means the most to you and God's people.

Honor physicians...for their gift of healing comes from the Most High. (Sirach 38:1,2)

Help me look at Your world with new eyes every day.

Wild about Wildlife

Dr. Lucy Spelman, the first woman director of the National Zoo in Washington, D.C., is passionate about pandas, as well as all animal life. She came by her love early, growing up in Connecticut with a menagerie that included cats, dogs, rabbits, goats and horses.

Spelman oversees the needs of 3500 creatures and 475 species, and her goal is to transform the 112-year-old zoo into an eco-conservation center with comfortable, natural animal habitats. "Animals in captivity deserve the absolute best care," she insists. "That's what motivated me to be a veterinarian. If a creature is to be impacted by humans, we have the technology and knowledge to give it an excellent quality of life."

We should never lose sight of the fact that we share the planet with all of God's creatures.

Take with you seven pairs of all clean animals...a pair of the animals that are not clean...seven pairs of the birds...to keep their kind alive...in seven days I will send rain. (Genesis 7:2,3,4)

Strengthen my compassion for all Your creation, Lord Jesus.

Slavery: An Honest Accounting

How much do we know about the institution of slavery?

While we know the economic benefits that slaves gave the South, we may forget that the North also profited from the enslavement of men, women and children from Africa. Many merchants, bankers and textile manufacturers who grew wealthy from their ties to the cotton trade were pro-slavery.

"On the eve of the Civil War, the economic value of slaves in the United States was $3 billion in 1860 currency, more than the combined value of all the factories, railroads and banks in the country," according to Columbia University historian Eric Foner.

"Much of the North's economic prosperity derived from what Abraham Lincoln, in his second inaugural address, called 'the bondsman's two hundred and fifty years of unrequited toil.'"

All Americans need to honestly examine the effect of slavery not only on our past, but on our present and on ourselves.

Let the oppressed go free and...break every yoke. (Isaiah 58:6)

Holy Spirit, guide us in repairing the damage slavery has done to our people and our nation.

A Proper Strategy

Veronica Chambers has discovered a secret to solo travel.

She is no amateur. She has studied in Morocco and Japan; enjoyed Madrid, Paris, Shanghai. Yet, she admits to being intimidated when friends want to know with whom she is traveling. "Oh," they say, with a mixture of surprise and pity.

But she has unearthed freedom in her solo adventures, and has no intention of changing. So, she brings along a prop: a camera which makes her pause and observe the details.

Books aren't as helpful. "As a somewhat shy person, my first line of defense is to reach for a book," she says. "But if I'd traveled through Marrakech with my head buried in a novel, I would have missed so much."

Whether planning exploits around the world or around the neighborhood on your own, remember that when you are in the thick of life, it isn't passing you by. Enjoy yourself.

Do not, therefore, abandon that confidence of yours; it brings a great reward. (Hebrews 10:35)

Thank You, God, for making me, me! Give me the confidence to enjoy my own company.

Tips on Helping Animals

"Suburban sprawl" has brought people and animals within close proximity of one another, sometimes perilously so.

Cec and Tom Sanders, who operate a wildlife rehabilitation center in Colorado, stress that people need to be educated about coexisting with wildlife. They suggest that if you find yourself confronting a critter in need of help, do not automatically "rescue" it since human contact can damage the animal's ability to live in the wild. Also, picking up or moving an animal may violate federal, state or local laws. Keep the number for the local fish-and-game warden or state wildlife agency handy.

Finally, remember that an injured animal can react violently or may be carrying a disease. Act carefully but caringly when trying to help and respect wildlife for the creatures they are.

God said, "Let the waters bring forth swarms of living creatures, and let birds fly above the earth...Let the earth bring forth living creatures of every kind...And God saw that it was good. (Genesis 1:20,24,25)

Bless our efforts, Father-Creator, to respect and preserve all forms of life.

A Sensitive Doctor's Approach

Kate Gadbois was used to being chastised by doctors.

Obese for most of her life, doctors' insensitive scare tactics didn't help her. Then she began treatment at Boston's Center for the Study of Nutritional Medicine run by Dr. George Blackburn. "I couldn't believe how different his thinking was," she says. "He didn't make me feel guilty. He treated it like a disease." His supportive, sensitive approach helped Gadbois lose weight.

All too aware that almost 100 million American adults are 20 or more pounds overweight, Blackburn not only combats fat but the tactlessness Gadbois and others frequently encounter. His workshops teach physicians how to better treat overweight patients. One of his favorite tools is the "fat empathy suit," a sand-filled bodysuit that doctors wear to learn to empathize with the extra weight obese patients carry.

When it comes to those dealing with problems, sympathy, empathy and understanding go a long way.

Be kind to one another, tenderhearted. (Ephesians 4:32)

Make me a reflection of Your empathy, Father.

Finding God

James Calvin Schaap, a writer in Sioux City, Iowa, lives on the prairie, "a place of vast horizons and few people." He has found a favorite spot 10 miles outside of town, a place named Highland. Although there is nothing there but a tiny cemetery, for Schaap the spot holds everything.

"I have no doubt that God is in the mountain-top experience," Schaap writes. "I feel His immensity most broadly in the expansive landscape that sits in its own reverent silence not far from my back door.

"Maybe it's the silence that draws me to Highland," he continues. "Whatever the reason, I go to this prairie place that is no more and I prefer to go alone so just for a moment I can stand humbly on a featureless, sweeping landscape. I stand and am still, knowing absolutely certain once again—He is God."

I will feed them on the mountains...I will feed them with good pasture, and the mountain heights of Israel shall be their pasture. (Ezekiel 34:13,14)

In the stillness, in the silence, You come to me, Father, drying my tears, filling me with joy.

Keeping Promises

Promises can be hard to keep, but the German village of Oberammergau has kept its word for almost 400 years.

In 1634, fearful that the bubonic plague would claim all their lives, the villagers gathered around the town cross and took a solemn oath to perform the "Play of the Suffering, Death and Resurrection of Our Lord Jesus Christ" every ten years.

The first performance was held at Pentecost in the village cemetery. Town records indicate that no one died of the plague after the villagers had made their promise.

Actors have to be natives of the village or longtime residents. Some have participated since they were infants. While there have been interruptions during times of war, spring of 2000 marked the 40th production of the passion play and over the season an estimated half a million spectators came to watch.

Be faithful to all your promises.

While we were enemies, we were reconciled to God through the death of His Son...(and we) will be saved by His life. (Romans 5:10)

Deliver us from unfaithfulness, Jesus, faithful Son of Torah.

Baseball's Lessons

Writer Bernie Sheahan is an avid baseball fan. But more than just hours of enjoyment, the game gives her lessons for life.

One player Sheahan admires is pitcher Orel Hershiser, now retired, because of his athletic skill and because he is never afraid to talk in public about his love for his wife and children and God. Sheahan found his remarks "eloquent and graceful."

Grace-full is what she means. "Baseball is nothing if not a game of grace, a forgiving sport that reminds us...there's always a next pitch, a next inning and a next game."

When you need sustenance during life's trials, remember baseball and the Bible. Sheahan, for instance, recalls the book of Lamentations: "His mercies are new every morning." Or, in the language of baseball, "there's always another season."

This I call to mind, and therefore I have hope: The steadfast love of the Lord never ceases, His mercies...are new every morning. (Lamentations 3:21-22,23)

Give us the strength to go on, God our refuge, no matter what.

Can Do Spirits

Benham, Kentucky, was a vibrant mining town during the early 20th century. But when International Harvester closed its plant in 1961, 600 residents were literally left with nothing.

Now, thanks to the hard work of a group of homemakers and retirees who named themselves the Benham Garden Club, Benham is thriving again. The turnaround began in 1991 when the women were asked to raise money for the down payment on a new fire truck. Their garage sale was such a success the garden club opened a thrift shop as a permanent fundraiser.

The 25 women in the club, including members of the town council, have used picnics and suppers to help refurbish parks, purchase police cars, and pay off the town's $47,000 debt. Next, the renovation of local historic buildings to enhance tourism.

Love for community and hard work have transformed the town. Every neighborhood could profit from such attention.

Hard work was created for everyone, and a heavy yoke is laid on the children of Adam. (Sirach 40:1)

Spur us on, Spirit, to better ourselves and our communities.

A Family Tradition

Broadcasting baseball games is the Caray family business.

First came the late Harry Caray, who enjoyed a legendary 53-year career. His son, Skip, is now in his 26th season of calling Atlanta Braves games, and the third generation of Carays in the broadcast booth, Chip, works Chicago Cubs games in the very same Wrigley Field booth as his grandfather did for so many years.

The three Carays only got to work together once, during a pre-game show. Chip was actually hired by the Cubs in 1998 to work with his grandfather, but Harry passed away before the season began. Chip says he constantly thinks about his grandfather, and now he dreams about working with his father someday—"just to have a chance to spend time with him."

Spend time with your family. Appreciate each other as unique individuals united by love as well as by blood.

I bow my knees before the Father, from whom every family...takes its name. I pray that...you may be strengthened in your inner being... through His Spirit. (Ephesians 3:14-16)

Help us cherish our families, God-Father.

To Your Health

More and more of those involved with health-care are interested in exploring so-called alternative medicine.

With the support of medical professionals, some patients are taking part in meditation and relaxation exercises. One doctor guides his 67-year-old patient, with breast cancer, in a relaxation exercise. The goal is to decrease her stress and buttress the body's immune system. As the patient exhales, she whispers "Jesus."

"While it hasn't exactly taken the medical profession by storm, there are signs that spiritual beliefs and practices are slowly working their way into the medical mainstream," according to Jeffery L. Sheler, writing in *U.S. News & World Report*.

And why not include mind, body and spirit in the service of health? These facets of the human person have been considered separately for too long. Appreciate your whole being.

I will lay sinews on you, and will cause flesh to come upon you, and cover you with skin, and put breath in you, and you shall live. (Ezekiel 37:6)

Thank You, God, for the gift of life.

Goodbye to a Deceased Father

Twenty years ago, Asia Wright's father, Jonathan Wright, was killed when an avalanche overwhelmed his climbing party in the Himalayas. Asia was only a baby at the time, but she has always wanted to know the father she has missed so terribly.

Mountaineer Rick Ridgeway had been with Wright on the icy slope that fateful day. "I'd had friends die on climbs, but I never held a friend in my arms while he died," Ridgeway recalls. Two decades later, he guided Asia Wright to her father's burial place on the mountain. "It was important for me to experience the places my father had been," said Asia.

Neither was prepared for the overwhelming feelings they experienced upon reaching the site of Wright's grave.

A daughter achieved a deeper appreciation of her father's adventurous spirit, and a friend renewed the vow made after the avalanche: to get the most out of every day.

So teach us to count our days that we may gain a wise heart. (Psalm 90:12)

I vow not to forget those no longer here, Maker.

Preserving the Star-Spangled Banner

Did you know that the original flag that inspired Francis Scott Key to compose our national Anthem, "The Star Spangled Banner," has become too fragile to display?

Smithsonian Institution officials now keep the flag in a glass case to protect it. And for more than two years, scientists, museum curators and conservators have been working to preserve the flag that flew over Fort McHenry.

It's lost a star and several yards of stripes during its long life, but, as Lawrence M. Small, secretary of the Smithsonian, put it, "Everything that those millions of flags flying across the United States stand for is symbolized in one flag–The Star-Spangled Banner. That is why the preservation of this national treasure has been a priority."

Respect and revere the flag, of course. But most importantly revere and preserve the rights and responsibilities of citizenship.

Bring good news to the oppressed...proclaim liberty to the captives, and release to the prisoners. (Isaiah 61:1)

Remind all citizens, Lord, that government derives its power from the free consent of the governed.

Dads Make a Difference

It's a fact that men today are more involved in childrearing. And just as there is something special between mothers and daughters, so too is the bond between father and son.

When fathers connect emotionally with sons, they are bestowing a wonderful gift, say psychologists. Take, for instance, 10-year-old Matt Kaminsky and his father, Tom. They do the usual "guy" things like throwing a football, or playing a little golf, or some hockey. But what Matt says he really likes about his dad is that they talk. "I don't know if anybody else talks to their dad like I do, but it's good to talk to my father. It's easy. I can ask him questions and everything."

Fathers, are you talking to your son every day? Are you sharing activities that show him the range of interests and emotions you have as a man?

Don't overlook the magnitude of your involvement in the lives of your sons and daughters. You won't get a second chance.

A son honors his father. (Malachi 1:6)

Father, inspire me to be a model to my children.

Brave in the Attempt

When one million athletes participate in 16,000 competitions in 150 countries that's got to be special. It is; the Special Olympics.

Begun in 1968, the program welcomes children and adults who are mentally retarded, offering them year-round training and competition. Athletes gain physical fitness and self-confidence, while families, volunteers and those who attend games get a keener appreciation of the abilities of those with particular challenges.

At one event, six young participants stood eagerly waiting for the 100-yard dash to begin. Just as the starting whistle sounded, one boy tripped, fell and began to cry. The other five stopped, and went back to help him up. Holding hands, they all crossed the finish line together to the cheers of the crowd.

The Special Olympics' oath is "Let me win. But if I cannot win, let me be brave in the attempt." May we all be so brave.

One in human form touched me and strengthened me. He said, "Do not fear, greatly beloved, you are safe. Be strong and courageous!" (Daniel 10:18-19)

Father, You embrace every one of Your children with love. Let me be eager to do the same.

Lessons from a Past Life

Pamela Thomas-Graham is president and chief executive of CNBC. Yet, she learned her most lasting skills and career success tips on her first job as a college student.

In an effort to earn her Harvard tuition, she took a job at a retail bookstore. Working with customers all day long helped her develop a keen memory as well as a tactful approach to dealing with people. "You have to work hard to understand customers' needs and make it easy for them," she explains.

Today, in television news and advertising sales, Thomas-Graham draws on all these skills. "I didn't know it would be paying off for this long," she says.

Take each and every experience in your life as an opportunity to learn. You may be surprised how and when the skills you pick up today will come in handy later.

Look closely and listen attentively. (Ezekiel 40:4)

May we value each and every life experience as a learning opportunity, or a chance to become a better person.

"You've Got Mail" and Math

When Vincent Krist's wife, Kristina, an eighth grade English teacher, had her laptop stolen, and with it all her student records, Krist came up with a way to help her and parents.

Krist started mygradebook.com, an online tool that he says is used by more than 70,000 parents and 600,000 students. Teachers store information on Web sites like Krist's, giving access to other teachers and to parents. Online data and e-mail alerts can include homework assignments, schedules of tests, and the latest rundown on a child's grades.

While some caution about privacy issues, others tout the technology's virtues. "It really takes the guesswork out of being a parent," says New Jersey mom Catherine Johnson, as she logs on to check her eighth-grade son Dan's homework assignments.

Unfortunately, even in the most loving, concerned families, some guesswork in inevitable. But good communication helps.

A disciple is not above the teacher. (Luke 6:40)

Father, help us teach others of Your great love and mercy.

Making People Comfortable

Wolfgang Zwiener says his job is to like people. "I make people comfortable," he says. "I spoil them if I can."

He has been a waiter at Brooklyn's Peter Luger Steak House for 38 years. The restaurant is a true original, opening in 1887 and still going strong. And so is Zwiener. He's the longest-serving waiter at the venerable establishment, and has been setting food on tables professionally since he was 18. Displaying a lifelong dedication to the art of food service, one of his regular customers calls him the "best waiter in America. He's personable and friendly, and he understands your needs."

For this man, putting smiles on the faces of others is the reward for long days and years spent serving hungry people.

Perform every job to the best of your ability, and enjoy it in the process.

Whoever serves must do so with the strength that God supplies, so that God may be glorified. (1 Peter 4:11)

Carpenter from Nazareth, help us be Your blessing to others.

A True Victor

Victor Rivers played football for Florida State under coach Bobby Bowden, and professionally for the Miami Dolphins. While not yet a household name, he has built a career as an actor, appearing in films with Eddie Murphy and Antonio Banderas. Yet he told a reporter recently that his proudest role is that of a survivor. Rivers grew up with an extremely abusive father.

Rivers' dramatic story includes turning to gang life after running away. When a football teammate's family took him in, Rivers saw that hope was possible. By his senior year in high school, he was captain of the team and class president.

Rivers says he no longer has a chip on his shoulder and now speaks out about domestic violence issues. "I learned what not to do as a human, as a man, and now as a father," he explains. "I use everything I learned to become a better person."

Use both the good and bad of your life to become a better, stronger human being.

Forgive us our debts, as we also have forgiven our debtors. (Matthew 6:12)

Almighty One, help us turn our pain into growth.

The Last of the Tallgrass Prairie

Along the Kansas Turnpike south of Emporia, prairie fires burn for miles, causing smoke dense enough to stall motorists.

Ranchers ignite these pastures every spring to clear out dried grass, kill encroaching trees and clear the way for new grass on which cattle will feast until winter.

But the last and largest remnant of the tallgrass praries that once covered more than a third of North America is about to be saved. The Prairie Passage, a newly designated national corridor more than 2,000 miles long, will mark the restoration and preservation of the once ubiquitous prairie. What's more, the effort will attempt to restore the wildflowers native to each section of the Passage, which will stretch from Texas to Minnesota.

Nature's beauty is not a given. It's a privilege and a treasure that we must honor, preserve and protect.

God said, "Let the earth put forth vegetation: plants yielding seed, and fruit trees...And God saw that it was good. (Genesis 1:11,12)

Lord, the beauty of Your earth is symbolic of Your love for us. May we never take it, or Your love, lightly.

Precious in His Eyes

If you have ever experienced the terrible feeling of being unloved or unlovable, consider Maya Angelou's words in her work, *Wouldn't Take Nothing for My Journey Now:*

"I began to sense that there might really be truth in the statement, 'God loves me', that there was a possibility that God really did love me. Me, Maya Angelou. I suddenly began to cry at the grandness of it all. I knew that if God loved me, then I could do wonderful things, I could try great things, learn anything. For what could stand against me with God, since one person, any person with God, constitutes the majority?"

What a beautiful way to view God's involvement in our lives. Each and every one of us does, truly, "matter" in the grand scheme of things.

You are precious in My sight, and honored, and I love you. (Isaiah 43:4)

Lord God, may I always remember that I am precious in Your sight.

Being a Great Parent

Writing in *Woman's Day*, Lori Erickson says, "There's no more important or difficult job than raising children...who are caring and responsible." She believes that parents need to impart necessary values to their children and offers ideas to help:

- Eat together as a family. Use the time to foster good feelings and enhance relationships.
- Limit TV and computer "screen time."
- Teach manners.
- Teach the value of a dollar.
- Let children occasionally fail. It will help them learn from their mistakes.

Erickson reminds us that a parent's "job isn't to win a popularity contest; it's to raise caring, capable adults." Mothers and fathers shouldn't try to be friends with their children. They are first, last and always, parents.

The Lord honors a father above his children...a mother's right over her children. (Sirach 3:2)

Guide and encourage parents, Creator.

Flying Octogenarians

Edna Lockwood of Goshen, Indiana, has 30 great-grandchildren and four great-great grandchildren. But what truly sets this remarkable 91-year-old apart is that she is one of only 30 pilots in the country who are 90 or older and authorized to fly. "I'm not out to set records," the flyer insists. "I just enjoy flying."

According to the FAA, pilots must undergo a flight review every two years. Actually, the oldest active pilot on record is Cole Kugel, 99, of Colorado, and Lockwood's friend, John Miller, flies at 95. He even talked Lockwood into joining an organization he heads, United Flying Octogenarians, for pilots 80 and older. When she hesitated to sign up, Miller urged her to "go for it."

Regardless of age, anyone can "go for it," as long as the mind and heart are engaged. Seize the moment and fly like an eagle.

Those who wait for the Lord shall renew their strength, they shall mount up with wings like eagles. (Isaiah 40:31)

Father, give me the courage not to allow time or age stand in my way.

Birding in the Big Apple

New York City is many things to many people, but few probably consider it a prime location for bird watching. Yet what is now a major metropolis has been on a main North-South migration route for tens of thousands of years. And its topography is attractively varied.

Marcia Fowle, co-author of *The New York Audubon Society Guide to Finding Birds in the Metropolitan Area,* in fact, calls the Big Apple ideal for "birding." That's because roughly 355 species of birds spend at least part of each year in New York City. Some migrate through, others nest for a while, and still others are full-time residents. Egrets, ibises and herons nest on Rikers Island. There are woodcocks in Pelham Bay Park. Falcons have their aeries on skyscrapers and tall apartment houses.

God's beautiful creatures, sights and sounds are everywhere. Watch for them.

By the streams the birds of the air have their habitation; they sing among the branches. (Psalm 104:12)

God, thank You for Your presence among us.

Pennies Make a Difference

It doesn't require wealth or prestige to make a difference in the world. All it takes is having a good heart and willing hands to do something for a community.

The children of New York know this.

Every year for a decade, hundreds of schools have taken part in a Penny Harvest with money going towards projects in their communities. After September 11, 2001, the collection was earmarked for victims of the attack on the World Trade Center.

The students of P.S. 133 in Park Slope, Brooklyn, know that helping others is a reward in-and-of-itself. Says, ten-year-old Elaine Vizcarra, "If you can help, you should." She also thinks she'd like to be a doctor so she can help folks in trouble.

The next time you think somebody else out there with more money, fame or time should be the one doing something for those in need, just remember the children who helped the greater good—one penny at a time.

The righteous give and do not hold back. (Proverbs 21:26)

Lord, help me be grateful for what You've blessed me with. Help me share with the less fortunate.

All Heart and Help

It's no wonder Lynne Totten has been honored as Michigan's top hospice volunteer.

She donates her time at a hospice in Gaylord, Michigan, comforting people who are dying and their families. In addition to offering patient care and grief counseling, she sews stuffed animals for the bereaved, using clothing from their deceased loved one. More than that, the volunteer acts as a speaker and fundraiser for the center. And for 20 years, she has also spread cheer in her role as a clown.

"She never says no," said volunteer manager Mary Weitzel.

At times, you may be consumed by your own daily problems and tend to forget the suffering of others. Rather than spending your time complaining about how tough life is, why not reach out to someone who could use your helping hand?

Depart from evil, and do good; so you shall abide forever. (Psalm 37:27)

Lord, give us the strength to share in the grief of others and not be consumed by our own suffering.

Harvesting Hope

When St. Frances de Sales parish in Lake Zurich, Illinois, got set to mark its 50th anniversary, many ideas were suggested to mark the milestone. One idea won: They would plant a farm.

Patches of potatoes, onions, zucchini, Swiss chard, carrots, corn, dill and more dot the 10-acre field. The food is donated to soup kitchens and food pantries in the area. Extra produce is sold Sunday mornings outside the church, with the money used for the farm's expenses and for seed money for next year's crop. Any excess funds from those sales are given to hunger-related charities.

"This has generated so much excitement," says George Koll, a pastoral associate. "People are using it to teach their kids about the growing cycle and about social justice. Parishioners are working shoulder to shoulder. It is a real faith sharing."

Looks like the greatest crops harvested at this farm are faith, hope and love.

Praise Him for His mighty deeds; praise Him according to His surpassing greatness!...Let everything that breathes praise the Lord! (Psalm 150:2,6)

May our lives and actions praise You, Father. May we thank You for Your many gifts to us.

Global Solutions Wanted

It's a harrowing thought: the continent that suffers most from the HIV-AIDS epidemic may not be able to afford even the reduced price antiretroviral drugs now available.

According to Peter Piot, a United Nations expert on HIV-AIDS, many Africans don't earn enough in a year to afford a year's supply of antiretroviral drugs, even at the reduced cost. There are worse problems: 95 percent of infected Africans don't know they have HIV-AIDS. Some people there even argue that HIV isn't the cause of AIDS.

"I'm angry all the time," Piot says. "Anger motivates me."

AIDS is a global problem. Its solution needs world and local efforts. Support education and research; volunteer to help those who are sick. Put your anger to work.

Rabbi, who sinned, this man or his parents, that he was born blind? Jesus answered, "Neither...he was born blind so that God's works might be revealed in him." (John 9:2-3)

I pray for those with HIV-AIDS, Lord. Help scientists and doctors find a cure. Help me do my part, too.

What's Love Got to Do with It?

What does love mean to you? The British apologist, professor and author, C.S. Lewis defined love with four Greek words: agape (loyal and benevolent concern for another's good); storge (the love of one's country), philia (the love between relatives) and eros (sexual love).

Wisdom can also be found in these responses from a group of four-through-eight-year-olds when asked that same question:

"Love is what makes you smile when you're tired."

"Love is when Mommy gives Daddy the best piece of chicken."

"When you love somebody, your eyelashes go up and down and little stars come out of you."

Perhaps the most powerful answer is this:

"God could have said magic words to make the nails fall off the cross, but He didn't. That's love."

Yes. It is.

No one has greater love than this, to lay down one's life for one's friends. (John 15:13)

Jesus, by Your living and by Your dying, You exemplify whole-souled love. Help us imitate You.

Summer Science

Ever wondered why people enjoy eating ice cream or riding roller coasters? So have researchers.

According to a *Newsweek* report, we're evolutionarily programmed to enjoy sweets. "In nature, bitter things are poisonous or spoiled. Sweet is the taste of carbohydrates, the body's fuel."

"During the plunge (of roller coasters)... dopamine floods the brain, giving...a high." Weightlessness feels great although "the sensation of your lunch also rising to the occasion does not."

According to researchers, the perfect landscape is "grassy rolling hills, small clusters of trees and a manicured lawn." A Texas A & M University psychologist says that scene gives us a sense of security, "easy access to food and low exposure to predators and disease."

Appreciate knowledge and, even more, wisdom.

Mortals...You have...crowned them with glory and honor. (Psalm 8:4,5)

Thank You, Creator, for all that it means to be human.

Home Is Where the Hot Dogs Are

On a day when most Americans were getting ready for backyard barbecues and parades down Main Street, Tom Dillehay, a University of Kentucky archeologist, was working in Peru – and feeling homesick for Fourth of July celebrations back home.

So the owners of a local restaurant decorated the place with red, white and blue flags. "They wanted to reach out to us, which was really wonderful," recalls Dillehay.

Independence Day festivities don't always take place on home soil. American workers in archeological sites around the world, for example, often make an effort to celebrate. For years, teams at two Etruscan sites have come together for possibly the only weenie roast ever celebrated in Chianti, Italy. After such an event, says excavation director Jane Whitehead, "One does not go to bed homesick."

Let your heart celebrate happy days, wherever you are.

They shall come trembling like birds from Egypt, and like doves from...Assyria; and I will return them to their homes, says the Lord. (Hosea 11:11)

May I look for You, Lord, in the moments of my day.

Honoring the Fallen

While browsing through some of the lesser-known street markets, Americans Rob Stiff and Jim Gain, who were on a business trip in Vietnam, were disturbed to find the dog tags of deceased American soldiers for sale.

To the Vietnamese field workers and vendors who had found them, they were simply debris from a war that had wasted their land. But Stiff and Gain knew that to American families, the identification tags were priceless reminders of their loved ones.

Several months later, the two men returned to Vietnam and bought the 640 tags they could find for $180. Back in the U.S. they compiled a Web site database of the names and ID numbers at www.founddogtags. com, to return the tags to the families of the dead. Ruth Decker's son, Lance Cpl. Allan George Decker, was killed in 1968. On receiving his tags she said, "I just hope that other families can find the kind of peace that I have felt today."

What can you do to help others find peace?

Blessed the peacemakers, for they will be called children of God. (Matthew 5:9)

Yahweh, make me an instrument of Your peace.

Looking Back to Look Ahead

Sometimes Independence Day threatens to become a whirl of picnics, parades and fireworks. History seems so distant; our freedom so inevitable. How could the American Revolution have gone any other way? But freedom has a price.

It's easy to forget the courage of so many, including the 56 signers of the Declaration of Independence who faced grave consequences. Twelve had their homes ransacked and burned. Seventeen lost everything they owned. Two lost sons in the war that followed the signing. Five were imprisoned. And fourteen paid the ultimate price: their lives (five after torture).

The Fourth of July is many things, including a memorial to those signers who had a vision for this country and made the sacrifices necessary to allow its future.

What have you done today to preserve our liberties?

You were called to freedom...do not use your freedom as an opportunity for self-indulgence. (Galatians 5:13)

How can we enhance the freedoms of all U. S. citizens, Author of our Liberties?

"Breathing Lessons"

Journalist Mark O'Brien died on Independence Day, 1999. He was 49 years old. Mr. O'Brien was no ordinary writer: he was an ordinary man forced to cope with extraordinary circumstances.

The subject of an Academy Award-winning documentary, "Breathing Lessons: The Life and Work of Mark O'Brien," he lived most of his life in an iron lung after boyhood polio.

As an adult, O'Brien lived as independently as possible. He attended the University of California at Berkeley and its Graduate School of Journalism. As a professional, he went from dictating his articles to using a mouth stick to operate a word processor. He founded a publishing house that specialized in poetry written by people with handicaps.

He credited his strong Roman Catholic faith with helping him deal with his disability.

As you face a problem, consider how significant it is in light of your faith.

The Lord God formed man...and breathed into his nostrils the breath of life. (Genesis 2:7)

Holy Spirit, inspire us.

Preserving Tradition

The Everett brothers, Randall and Roger, still sponsor free Saturday night bluegrass concerts at their old home place in Suwanee, Georgia, as they've done since the 1960s.

The brothers started the concerts as a way to help their parents deal with the death of their police officer brother. They taught themselves to play guitar and banjo and invited neighbors to join them. By 1970, they needed more room and built a barn and furnished it with old church pews.

The popular concerts preserve something of the South's rural past and provide entertainment for families to enjoy together. "Everything has changed so much," said Randall Everett. "But we play the music just the way we did when we started."

Giving joy and comfort to others won't ever go out of style.

Wine and music gladden the heart, but the love of friends is better than either. (Sirach 40:20)

Bless my friends, Jesus.

The Ecuador Hat?

Perhaps you're familiar with the pride of many a haberdashery—the clean, crisp Panama hat, long a favorite of the well-dressed man.

What may surprise you is that genuine Panama hats are crafted, as they have always been, in Ecuador. The stylish straw hat that was all the rage among gold seekers crossing Panama in the 1800s had been created from toquilla, a palmlike plant which grows wild not far from Ecuador's coast.

Like the Panama hat, which might better be called the Ecuador hat, things are not always what they seem. Labels can be misleading; appearances, too, however widely used and accepted they may be.

Learn not to judge people by appearances or labels but by themselves.

Do not judge by appearances, but judge with right judgment. (John 7:24)

Lord, teach me that a person's heart, character and spirit are what matter. Help me always be wary of stereotypes.

Go With the Flow

Have you ever walked along a rocky beach and stopped to gaze into a tidal pool? Children and adults seem fascinated with the deceptively calm water teeming with life. However, what oftentimes go unseen are the biological and physical stresses on the tidal pool's inhabitants.

The summer sun can heat a pool 20 to 30 degrees in less than a day. Water evaporates, causing the salt concentration in the seawater to increase. Depending on the balance between plant and animal life, oxygen can be depleted.

All through these stresses, the tide pool's inhabitants–hermit crabs, marine bugs and worms, algae, barnacles and mussels–thrive, adapting to each and every change nature throws their way.

Life insistently and constantly challenges us. We can be resistant or we can be willing to adapt and thrive.

I the Lord do not change; therefore you...have not perished. (Malachi 3:6)

You have blessed us with life and all its complexities, dear Father. Let us be accepting of Your will.

Changing the World, One Child at a Time

Cincinnati's Mattie Johnson may operate a small candy and convenience store, but what she really offers her community is advice. Well-known in her neighborhood, kids straighten up when they see her. "Good afternoon, Miz Mattie," they say with their best manners. Mattie Johnson is a role model to be respected, based on her many acts of kindness.

The shop, called Grandma's Hands, is really an esteem-building program for young women. Besides offering low-priced snacks, the store serves as a workspace for creating cloth tote bags, quilts and aprons to sell or give away. And teenage girls have a safe haven in which to learn about cooking, sewing and fending for themselves from volunteers.

"We were worried...So many...were having babies, and they weren't much more than babies themselves," says Miz Mattie. She has never missed a day at the little store. "I wake up, think about the children and out the door I go," she says.

As an individual, you are an important part of the solution to the world's problems. What can you do, today, now?

Sustain in me a willing spirit. (Psalm 51:12)

Inspire me to good deeds, Savior.

The Donkey in the Well

A legend tells of a farmer's donkey who fell down into a well. The farmer realized that getting him out would be virtually impossible. Resigned to that fact, he invited all his neighbors to come over and help him shovel directly into the well, effectively burying his donkey.

At first, the donkey, realizing what was happening, cried. Then, to everyone's amazement, he quieted down. A few shovel loads later, the farmer looked down the well and was astonished by what he saw. With every shovel of dirt that hit his back, the donkey would shake it off and take a step up. Pretty soon, everyone was amazed as the donkey stepped up over the edge of the well and trotted off.

The lesson from this tale? Life is going to shovel dirt on you–all kinds of it. The trick is shake it off–and take a step up.

Come to Me, all you that are weary and are carrying heavy burdens, and I will give you rest. Take My yoke upon you, and...you will find rest for your souls. (Matthew 11:28-29)

When the cares of the day weigh me down, Lord, I turn to You, for hope and consolation.

Creativity and Children

Sandra Byrd, author of the *Secret Sisters* book series and the mother of two, offers some creative activities for children.

Flashlight Bear Hunt. Hide all of your children's stuffed animals around the yard. After dark, give each child his or her own flashlight and send them out on an "animal rescue mission." Help them find all the animals.

Zoo Photo Safari. Turn a routine visit to the zoo into a special one by buying a disposable camera for each child and then sending them out on a photo safari. Teach them how to take the best photo of each animal. Afterwards, put the photos in an album.

Dino Dig. Boil some chicken bones clean and bury them–not too deeply–in the backyard. Then equipped with a spade or a spoon, an old toothbrush and a cookie sheet, set your junior paleontologists loose to collect and clean their "dinosaur" bones.

Be innovative. Encourage others to be so.

Let the little children come to Me...it is to such as these that the kingdom of God belongs. (Mark 10:14)

Creator, show parents how to teach their children.

Guardian Angels

At a Long Island harbor, pier employees Eric Svihovec and Chris Crociata were seeking cover from a torrential downpour. But through the driving rain, they saw a car plunge from a boat ramp 100 feet away.

Emily Wardell had been driving through sheets of rain with her two-month-old baby, Olivia, strapped into a rear safety seat. She was looking for her husband whose boat was caught in the storm. Blinded by the rain, Wardell failed to stop the car in time.

Within seconds the men dove into the harbor. As Svihovec pulled Wardell out she screamed that Olivia was still in the back seat. Together, they pulled on the jammed seat, but the baby's head went under water. With one last furious yank, Svihovec tore the seat free and held the baby overhead as Crociata whisked Olivia to the pier.

Wardell calls them "my guardian angels" and says they restored her "faith in humanity."

Look closely. Heroes are all around us. Even you.

Be courageous and valiant. (2 Samuel 13:28)

May my heart, head and hands be strong, Spirit of God.

Different Drums

Combining European opera with Native American drums might not have occurred to many.

But it did to Libby Moore, a Spokane native and the artistic director of The Other Company, a small musical company. She asked the Kalispel Indians of Usk, Washington, to create an adaptation of Mozart's *The Magic Flute*. The elders agreed.

Opera professionals from Spokane, Seattle and New York began working with Stanley Bluff Jr., the tribe's education coordinator. The production is narrated in English and Kalispel. The Frog Island Drummers and Singers, in native dress, formed the chorus.

"It's like anything else in life, I guess," said Bluff. "You're never going to grow unless you step out of your comfort zone."

Do you step out of your comfort zone?

O Lord of hosts, happy is everyone who trusts in You. (Psalm 84:12)

Let us uncover the riches You have for us, Almighty One.

Letters: Lost and Found

If you still haven't received the birthday card your cousin told you was in the mail, it might just be a "nixie." A nixie is what the post office calls correspondence without an address sufficient to get it where it's going or a return address to get it back to the sender. Still, there's a chance the mail will get through.

When letters and packages are scanned and rejected by the post office's optical character readers, other sensors try to interpret the address. If they fail, humans with expert knowledge of geography, buildings, etc. attempt to solve the mail mystery. Only then are undeliverable pieces sent to a dead-mail center where, after 90 days, they are destroyed or auctioned if they contain valuables.

Everyone needs a second or third—or more—chance at some time. Be willing to offer that chance to others, too.

Be merciful, just as your Father is merciful. (Luke 6:36)

Jesus, You offer forgiveness and hope to us again and again and again. Teach me to do the same for my neighbors.

Free Carrying Case Included

Lynn Goodman-Strauss wanted to help the largely homeless population of day laborers in her home city of Austin, Texas. She knew they were going to physically exhausting jobs without breakfast, but she couldn't see how best to feed them.

It had to be something she could prepare in large quantities, something safe, nutritious, affordable, easy to eat, well-liked...the list went on.

She prayed for guidance. It came.

Now known throughout Austin as the "Egg Lady," Goodman-Strauss can be found most mornings on street corners in the neighborhoods where day laborers are picked up, dispensing hardboiled eggs for the struggling workers. One of God's simplest creations is helping her to change lives.

There is something simple you can do to help others today.

Be rich in good works, generous, and ready to share. (1 Timothy 6:18)

Show me, Great Teacher, how to use Your whole world to help others.

A Better World, One Child at a Time

Every year, on Dr. Seuss's birthday, you can find Will Shields in a Cat in the Hat topper reading to children at the St. Vincent Family Service Center in Kansas City.

Doing something for people in need is an everyday activity for the star offensive lineman for the National Football League's Chiefs. His "Will to Succeed" Foundation helps abused and neglected women and children. Widely respected for his community service, he is a hands-on volunteer who supports charities with his participation, as well as his donations. Sr. Berta Sailer, assistant director of St. Vincent's, says, "He gives you the resources, but he also gives you the time."

Will Shields simply asks, "Why not try to do things to help, because these are the kids that are going to run the world someday?"

What's your answer? Help someone, somehow, today.

A disciple whose name was Tabitha...was devoted to good works and...charity. (Acts 9:36-37)

Generous Father, show me how to share the gifts and talents with which You have blessed me with others.

A Drastic Solution

Steve and Karen Porath watched as their dream house burned to the ground. Yet, as Karen said, intentionally destroying it was a relief, for "that house almost killed our child."

The Poraths' house was contaminated with black mold, a toxic fungus that feeds on moisture and thrives in damp areas. Two days after bringing their newborn son, Mitchell, home from the hospital, the baby became violently ill. He developed a rash and constant infections, and doctors were baffled. Almost a year later, the Poraths had the house tested for contaminants, and that's when the high levels of mold were discovered. The family never entered the house again and enlisted volunteer firefighters to burn it down, with all their belongings inside.

The Poraths are struggling to put their lives back together, but Karen is optimistic that something good can come of the horrible experience. "We're starting over. If Steve and I can make it through this, we'll have the strongest marriage ever."

Every family faces challenges. Face them together.

Deliverance belongs to the Lord! (Jonah 2:9)

Help me to bear the heaviest of burdens, Savior.

An Unexpected Gift

Time was running out for Hal Smith.

The athletic director at Malone College in Ohio was on the waiting list for a liver transplant. Then one day, his wife called to say that Sharon Looney, a Malone softball coach, "wants to donate part of her liver." Smith had heard about living-donor transplants, in which a healthy person donates a section of his or her liver.

He did not know her well, but he immediately went to her office and asked her, "Are you sure you want to do this?"

Two years later, Looney says she was "as sure as I had been about anything." Smith, who cannot talk about Looney's gesture without choking up, says, "Sharon gave me a gift I will never be able to repay."

Extend yourself to assist a person in need. Your reward will be immeasurable.

You gave me food...and...something to drink... you welcomed me...you gave me clothing ...you took care of me...and you visited me. (Matthew 25:35,36)

Jesus, enable me to follow Your example of selflessness.

A Victory for Dad

Millions were saddened and moved by the tragic death of racing legend Dale Earnhardt, who was killed in a crash at Florida's Daytona International Speedway. Amazingly, his son, Dale Earnhardt, Jr., not only entered the Pepsi 400 race at the same track a mere five months after his father's death, he won it.

Earnhardt, Jr. conceded that the first lap or two of practice at the Speedway was tough, but he nevertheless was able to put aside memories of his father and complete a storybook finish. Stuck behind five cars with six laps to go, he weaved in and out and sealed the victory. Afterwards, with a sense of relief, he said, "I wanted to hug everybody. It really got me back to normal."

Our loved ones never truly leave us. Dale Earnhardt, Jr., dedicating his victory to his dad, said it best: "My father was with me tonight."

However painful our grief, love is stronger, if we let it be.

Honor your father and your mother. (Mark 7:10)

Be with me and my loved ones, Sacrificial Lamb.

A Bluesman Celebrates

He's one of the last of his kind, for as Pinetop Perkins puts it, "I'm a bluesman, through and through." In fact, to celebrate his 88th birthday, Perkins awed a crowd at a Chicago club when the master of "electric blues" sat down at the piano and performed.

According to many aficionados, Perkins has become an icon in the blues world, but not without enduring his own woes. Born and raised in the Deep South, Perkins spent years as a studio and backup musician, only embarking on a solo career when he was in his 70's. In the mid 1990's, however, with the death of his wife and drinking more than ever, Perkins was in trouble. But he didn't give up on himself. He completed a 12-step rehabilitation program and began performing again.

Today, Pinetop Perkins' date book is full, and, he says, "I can't retire even if I want to. Everybody's calling me."

It's never too late to overcome pain and lead a rich life.

In Me you may have peace. In the world you face persecution. But take courage; I have conquered the world! (John 16:33)

Help me find music in my life, Master.

I Resign!

Why do youngsters yearn to grow up and adults for the irresponsibility of youth? One overwhelmed adult said this:

"I am hereby officially tendering my resignation as an adult...I would like to accept the responsibilities of an 8-year-old again. I want to go to McDonald's and think that it's a four star restaurant. ...

"I want to think M&Ms are better than money because you can eat them. I want to return to a time when...all you knew was to be happy because you were blissfully unaware of all the things that should make you worried or upset.

"I want to think the world is fair, that everyone is honest and good. ...I want to believe in the power of smiles, hugs, a kind word, truth, justice, peace, dreams, the imagination, mankind, and making angels in the snow. ...Here's my checkbook and my car keys, my credit card bills and my 401K statements."

We do grow up. Time gives us adult responsibilities. But don't be afraid to take a break to refresh yourself.

When I became an adult, I put an end to childish ways. (1 Corinthians 13:11)

Give me the strength to be an adult, Lord of life.

Talking without Words

Sarah Collier, 17, has Muscular Dystrophy. She speaks about her hereditary nerve disorder to help others to understand her disease. She also volunteered for a summer at a center for adults with developmental disabilities. There, she met Mason.

"Mason and I would go for walks, or color," she says. "Talking was the hardest part, because Mason has autism, a neurological disorder...While Mason can speak, he rarely does. But soon we formed a bond."

Sarah continued to see Mason after that summer. "People with autism are often classified as being trapped within themselves," she says. "But Mason made me believe you must work to figure out how to reach them."

Mason also taught Sarah about "the power of a certain look or a friendly pat on the shoulder," she explains. "Service," Sarah adds, "makes your heart bigger." Make your heart bigger. Serve God's people.

Show by your good life that your works are done with gentleness born of wisdom. (James 3:13)

Spirit give me the words I need to help others come to know You.

More than One Thing at a Time?

Scientists may have bad news for "multi-taskers" who think they can do more than one complex activity at one time.

A recent study using magnetic resonance imaging has revealed that the brain isn't well suited to doing more than one complex task at once.

When drivers try to navigate heavy traffic and talk on a cell phone, for example, brain activity doesn't double. Instead, brain activity is split between the two tasks. Neither one is done as well as it could be were it was the sole object of concentration.

Although, the study did not directly test those who drive and talk on the phone at the same time, it did test tasks that affected similar areas of the brain.

This study seems to confirm what many people knew: to do something really well you have to focus.

Pay attention to what you hear. (Mark 4:24)

Who—and what—needs my attentive concern, Jesus?

A Master of Shorts

In the summer of 2001, Eudora Welty died at the age of 92. Her short stories, notable for their imagery, sharp dialogue and fierce wit, were often set against the backdrop of the South.

Born in 1909 in Jackson, Mississippi, Welty credits her parents for her devotion to books. She found her ability to tell a story in her skill to listen for one, she said.

She was a writer for radio and newspapers, a Pulitzer Prize winner and the author of numerous stories, novels, essays and book reviews. In her 1984 memoir, Welty wrote: "My continuing passion would not be to point the finger in judgment but to part a curtain, that invisible shadow that falls between people, the veil of indifference to each other's presence, each other's wonder, each other's human plight."

Open your mind and heart when you listen to another. Be willing to hear what that person says, not just your interpretation.

Do not condemn, and you will not be condemned. (Luke 6:37)

For all in need this day, Master, give them strength, send them Your love through us.

Afloat and Safe

Two teenaged boys basked in the warmth of the sun and enjoyed idle conversation as they splashed on a homemade raft off the shores of Lake Erie. Eventually, they drifted out farther than they had intended.

The boys tried several ways of returning to shore on the raft, to no avail. Finally, one of the boys directed the other to abandon the raft. "We either swim for shore now or they'll have to send the Coast Guard for us later," Tim cautioned.

Completely spent as he approached the shore, Tim called for help from his brother who was on the dock. Tad leapt into the water only to discover it was but waist deep.

"Stand up!" Tad cried. The two teens had been out of danger for some time but didn't know it.

Where are you struggling unnecessarily in your life? Trust God's aid and give yourself to Him.

The yoke of their burden, and the bar across their shoulders, the rod of their oppressor, You have broken as on the day of Midian.
(Isaiah 9:4)

Help me, Loving God, to act in the security of Your love.

Art and Soul

There is a strong revival in traditional Hispanic arts in New Mexico. In fact, Santa Fe's annual Spanish Market, held at the end of July, has grown from 35 to over 170 exhibitors since 1982.

Furniture makers, weavers, tinsmiths and artists gather to make a wide array of their works available. "Poor man's gold is among them."

Using a technique handed down from family to family, artists work with straw until it is smooth and lustrous, then inlay it in wooden religious items.

"Designed for homes and churches, these images were at once utilitarian and deeply religious," writes Patricia Leigh Brown in the *New York Times,* "a vibrant blend of the everyday and the miraculous."

As believers our lives should always reflect a vibrant blend of the mundane and the miraculous.

**Do not forget the Lord your God.
(Deuteronomy 8:11)**

We celebrate Your presence in the everydayness of our lives, Holy One.

When You Least Expect It...

If you've ever taken antibiotics for an illness, it is likely you never imagined that more than 1600 years ago, someone could have done the same.

Anthropologist Debra Martin discovered in the mummified remains of a Sudanese person that tetracycline, an antibiotic introduced in the 1950s, had already been available as a result of the Egyptian and Nubian methods of brewing beer.

The discovery was an accident. Martin was doing routine research when she simply used the available microscope which used ultraviolet light, thus revealing the presence of tetracycline in human bone matter.

Life often presents its greatest challenges and opportunities when we least expect them. Being open to discovery can make all the difference in your life and in the lives of others.

Be alert at all times. (Luke 21:36)

Holy Spirit, help me keep an open mind and spirit.

Fighting for a Cause—and for Both Sides

A typical day for attorney Diann Rust-Tierney sometimes includes attending a candlelight vigil in front of the Supreme Court or working to help death row defendants.

Rust-Tierney would have it no other way. Since the 1980s, she has been opposed to capital punishment because "everyone is precious in the eyes of the Creator."

She is unique in her fight, however, in that she has taken the time to listen to and understand the position and feelings of proponents of the death penalty: "It's often lost, but we are angry and grieving for the victims of these crimes, as well as angry over what the state does to the defendants."

Supporting a cause can be a worthwhile pursuit. Becoming overzealous, or losing sight of others' opinions, can dilute your message. Whatever your beliefs, try to take time to hear the "other side of the story." That could help you get closer to a solution.

Act with justice and righteousness.
(Jeremiah 22:3)

Help me keep an open mind, Lord.

Siblings Raising Siblings

There are some 140,000 households nationwide in which older siblings are raising younger siblings.

Twin 18-year-old sisters Chanthan and Chantha Khiev of Oakland, California, are the primary caretakers of their twin brothers, Joshua and Nicholas. Their mother, Khorn, died at 43 after giving birth to the twins. She left eight children.

With the help of social workers, dedicated teachers and their community, the young women are getting by. They're balancing and meeting the challenges of schoolwork with motherhood as best they can. Chantha says, "sometimes I want to hold the babies so tight, and sometimes I don't want to hold them at all. But I miss them when I'm at school."

Many people have obligations thrust on them—ready or not. The best thing you can do is simply the best you can.

Let us love one another. (1 John 4:7)

Jesus, help family members care for each other.

Book It!

Seattle Librarian Nancy Pearl wanted to bring people together through books. Armed with a small grant, she launched a program to encourage the entire city of Seattle to simultaneously read Ernest Gaines' "A Lesson Before Dying." It was a smash success. People read the book, which deals with racial prejudice, and then met with others to discuss it.

"It's based on the noble idea of community," says Pearl. She wanted to bring together people who would not otherwise have a reason to meet.

Other cities are following suit. In Chicago, which selected *To Kill a Mockingbird,* discussion groups were organized by places from museums to coffee shops.

According to Claudia Durst Johnson of the University of Alabama, "anything that causes people to think and interact and maybe even figure out how other people feel is a great thing."

Reading and thinking go hand in hand.

Brothers and sisters, do not be children in your thinking; rather...be adults. (1 Corinthians 14:20)

Show us new ways, Loving God, to build community.

Not Giving in to Cynicism

Despite their reputation as hard and heartless, New Yorkers can be soft touches.

Problem is, once-in-a-while, they, like Good Samaritans everywhere, can be duped.

James Daly, a disabled veteran, made headlines when he reported that he was mugged and his wheelchair stolen. After New Yorkers had responded with an outpouring of generosity, the police discovered that Daly had concocted the story because he wanted a newer, better wheelchair, as well as help in obtaining a new home.

More often than not, however, someone's cry for help is genuine. There's a difference between caution and cynicism, so don't give up on others, just use your best judgment.

A priest...passed by...likewise a Levite...But a Samaritan...when he saw him, he was moved with pity...and bandaged his wounds.
(Luke 10:31,32,33,34)

No matter the risk, help us reach out to help others, Jesus.

Life Experiences

When he was only eight years old, Michael Van Rooyen watched his mother die of melanoma. He knew then that he wanted to be a doctor. When he was a teen, he volunteered with a disaster relief team. And he also knew he would continue in that work.

Today, Dr. Van Rooyen is the founding director of the Johns Hopkins Center for International Emergency, Disaster, and Refugee studies. His hours are spent in fields of despair and war in places like Kosovo, Rwanda, Bosnia and El Salvador. He has contracted various diseases and has even been held hostage for the sake of his work. Why? His goal is "trying to help people in the worst situations."

Life experiences help shape our lives as they did Van Rooyen's. But we control how we interpret their effect. Will they motivate us for evil or for good? For despair or hope?

So teach us to count our days that we may gain a wise heart. (Psalm 90:12)

Yahweh, it is sometimes difficult to put my life in perspective. Let me stand outside of myself to see more clearly.

A League of Their Own

When Bryan Hall whacked a ball into the outfield at the new Conyers, Georgia, baseball field, players cheered wildly. "You hit the ball all the way to the fence!" a coach enthused. "That was amazing!" It was. Bryan and his teammates all have disabilities.

Thanks to Gary Garner, whose daughter, Lindsay, has muscular dystrophy, these youngsters have their own league and specially designed playing field. Garner, an electrical contractor thought of the idea when a friend mused about how nice it would be for their sidelined kids to be on a team.

Now the Miracle League boasts more than 150 youngsters aged 5 to 18. Each plays with an able-bodied buddy who may help swing a bat or run an athlete in a wheelchair to base. This new "field of dreams" was built for all the right reasons because "it's not about winning, it's about getting to play," says Garner.

So much of life is about overcoming barriers. Lend a hand to anyone who could use your assistance and kindness.

**(Put) no obstacle in anyone's way.
(2 Corinthians 6:3)**

Despite difficulties, help me to persevere, Lord God.

Winning Big at the Little World's Fair

Every year for more than a century, summer in Grahamsville, New York, has meant much more than warm weather. It's the home of the Little World's Fair. Here local 4-H clubs show off their prized animals including cows, chickens, ducks, sheep, and goats for competition.

Consider what 15-year-old Robert Kautz, whose Netherland Dwarf rabbit won best in breed, says about his experience at the Fair: "I like rabbits...you have to work with them every day. ...I was happy I did so well in my first year. I think I have a future."

Youth groups can offer more than just activities to young people, they can help foster responsibility and achievement. Consider volunteering your time and talent to the young. Give them a future.

The Lord was my support. (Psalm 18:18)

Watch over the young, Lord God, so they may have guidance and protection.

A Quiet Activist

Florida's Everglades, and the plant and animal species that live there, are dying of thirst. Mary Barley is trying to end that.

Barley heads Save Our Everglades, a group started by her late husband, George, who was killed in a plane crash six years ago. Embracing his legacy, Barley is the public face of the biggest environmental rescue mission in U.S. history. She is striving to ensure that the state and federal governments fulfill their commitments, and her vigilance shows no sign of letting up.

Her husband's death was "the most defining moment in my life," says Mary Barley. "His life force was so positive. What is life if you don't live it? I learned that even pain and agony is life."

In the wake of grief and suffering, a purpose in life can present itself. Stay open to the gift of life and its possibilities.

Grief may result in death, and a sorrowful heart saps one's strength. ...Do not give your heart to grief...you do the dead no good, and you injure yourself. (Sirach 38:18,20,21)

May purpose and peace of mind be mine, Father.

Mother Teresa's Fingerprints

After a brief meeting with Mother Teresa in Calcutta a number of years ago, Jim Towey was sent to visit Sister Luke at the Missionaries of Charity's Home for the Dying.

There, Towey said: "I saw people who didn't have sophisticated medical care, but…what people want the most–their dignity." On his return home, this Washington, D.C. resident continued his connection to Mother Teresa's community by becoming a volunteer. He also provided free legal counsel.

Committed to help everyone age and die with dignity, he founded Aging With Dignity, which promotes "Five Wishes," a living will that lets loved ones know how you want to spend your final days.

Show respect for your family and yourself: make a will. Consider practical issues related to health and finances. Above all, think about the legacy of love you can leave behind.

There is a season, and a time for every matter under heaven: a time to be born, and a time to die. (Sirach 3:1-2)

All my days, Master, You are with me, showering me with Your love and showing me Your way.

3,000 Teddy Bears Send Comfort

When Justin Flagg and his twin siblings, April and Travis, heard about the World Trade Center tragedy in New York City, they knew they wanted to help, and they knew exactly how.

Realizing they were too young to donate blood or money, the youngsters from Bertram, Texas, decided to send their own stuffed animals. That became a class project, then a school project, and then a project of their entire county.

When the Flagg family traveled east, with them came the 3,000 teddy bears they had collected to comfort the children of victims. Each of the bears came with a note written by the donor. One read, "My arms are too short to reach to New York, so I'm sending you this hug."

People of all ages are vital to our society. Treating young people with respect will contribute to their self-confidence and ultimately, their ability to improve and rebuild our society.

Do justice...love kindness (Micah 6:8)

God, bless the youth of our nation, so they may know they have a purpose and a mission in Your eyes.

Poetry in Stone

Dan Snow has seen "a lot more fences and walls going up in the past 10 years" in his Vermont county. He attributes this to rising property values. Maybe that's because he's one of the last builders of dry or unmortared stone walls in the area.

After 25 years of training with master wall builders, Snow is renowned for his own intricate creations, in which he takes oddly shaped rocks, stones and even small pebbles to construct some of the most beautiful, stately dry stone walls and grottos in New England. What he enjoys most is using rocks and stones that have been "recycled" from previous structures to create new walls. "I think this stone has gotten prettier every time it's used," he says.

What unusual talents do you possess? What may seem quirky or unusual may be a golden treasure in the eyes of someone else. Cultivate your talents and interests, however small or unconventional.

We have gifts that differ according to the grace given to us. (Romans 12:6)

God, thank You for all of the gifts You've given me.

History, Progress, on the Rails

The Ravenswood Line of Chicago's rapid transit system, begun in 1907, is one of America's oldest elevated transit lines still running intact.

For just $1.50, the full 60-minute roundtrip offers a look into the Chicago that used to exist, as well as the very different, new North Side that will take its place.

Some regard the Ravenswood Line as an unlikely survivor in a time when most of the elevated trains in the nation have been replaced by subways, ground-level trains, or even, freeways. Yet, the character and beauty of the train continues to attract riders. In fact, some city developers believe the train contributes to the area's rebirth, bringing new riders and residents.

What has changed in your community? What things would you like to see preserved? What will you do about it?

I will...teach you the way you should go. (Psalm 32:8)

Give us the wisdom to choose and use ecologically sound mass transit systems, Creator.

All Is Not Lost at Sea

How safe are you when you go boating?

U.S. Coast Guard Petty Officer Harry Craft says that "you'd better be able to take care of yourself if the craft gets into trouble." He recommends keeping these items on board in case of emergencies at sea: glow sticks, inflatable vests, a waterproof three-mile strobe light, and a small signal mirror.

If you do end up adrift, George Cavallo of the Coast Guard's Rescue Swimmers suggests creating a makeshift anchor out of extra rope and a bucket or roll of clothing to buffet the waves. If you're in the water, put on all available clothing to retain body heat. And use your imagination, Cavallo advises: "I once helped find a guy who was using the hologram on his credit card to reflect the sun."

Exercise caution in any potentially dangerous situation.

A windstorm swept down...they were in danger. They...woke Him up, shouting, "Master, Master, we are perishing!" And He...rebuked the wind and...waves...and there was a calm. (Luke 8:23,24)

Jesus, watch over me and keep me safe.

Keeping His Eyes on the Prize

It was no ordinary day for Joe Parker when he was prepping his 3-year-old filly, Logan's Girl, for what would be his first career victory as a racehorse trainer.

When Logan's Girl won a six-furlong, $40,000 race at Belmont Park, she brought Parker's years-long dream to fruition. He had come to the United States from Trinidad in 1972 and got a job as walker at Aqueduct race track. Eventually, he worked his way up to groom and then assistant under accomplished trainers.

Although Parker is still considered a rookie trainer and runs just a fledgling operation, he takes his small-time status good-naturedly, keeps things in perspective, and never gives up his dream. "This is the sport of kings, and one day I'll get (back) in that winner's circle."

We all have our dreams. Stay focused on them.

The one who endures to the end will be saved. (Mark 13:13)

Jesus, I am not always able to persevere. Please help me walk the path You set out for me, with joy and willingness, every step of the way.

Never Say Never

U.S. Congressman Jim Langevin calls himself an optimist. "I always see the possibilities," he says. "It would bother me more not to try than to try and fail."

His attitude helped him be elected to Rhode Island's legislature while still a college senior. It spurred him to earn a master's in public administration at Harvard University. And it continues to give him a voice on such issues as gun control, health insurance, and education.

These issues matter to Langevin. As a teenager, he spent a summer vacation working with the local police department. That year, as SWAT team members examined a hand gun it accidentally discharged. The bullet hit a metal locker and then Langevin's neck and spinal cord. He was paralyzed from the chest down.

One of his hopes today? "To inspire other people not to give in to limitations."

We can't control everything that happens to us, but we can always control our attitude.

Hope does not disappoint us. (Romans 5:5)

Keep us focused on our potential, Spirit of Fortitude.

The Welcoming Water

Many things in his Perth Amboy, New Jersey, hometown have changed over the years, says writer Alan Cheuse. But the impact of the local waters, particularly the Raritan Bay, on townspeople's lives has remained constant.

"Water attracted the first human inhabitants... nomadic groups of Lenni Lenape (or Delaware) Indians," wrote Cheuse. "Water drew the Swedish crews who sailed into the bay in the early 1600s and made their way to both sides of the Delaware River. And water later drew the Dutch sailors and traders who settled on the island of Manhattan."

Hundreds of years later, Cheuse and his boyhood friends swam and chased horseshoe crabs in bay waters; walked on piers and rented rowboats. Today, there is a newly restored waterfront and locals still spend time by it.

Enjoy water's power to refresh and restore.

You make springs gush forth. (Ps. 104:10)

Lord, may we fully appreciate and protect water, a miracle in our midst.

Garden of Hope and Remembrance

At the southern tip of Manhattan, gardens have provided a green oasis to those who live or work or walk through Battery Park City. Much of the soil was taken from the excavation for the World Trade Center.

After the WTC buildings were destroyed on September 11, 2001, horticulturist Eric Fleisher and his crew removed debris and ash using vacuum cleaners, hoses, rakes and shovels. Underneath, waiting to be tenderly coaxed back to vibrancy, they found dahlias, impatiens, salvia, and more.

One of the first areas dug out and cleaned was the garden's Police Memorial. Gardeners worked to replace the ugliness with beauty. They added a new plant to the border, a sedum appropriately called Autumn Joy.

However difficult, work to answer evil with goodness.

There is hope for a tree, if it is cut down, that it will sprout again...though its root grows old...and its stump dies...yet at the scent of water it will bud and put forth branches. (Job 14:7,8,9)

Keep us hope-filled, Mighty Lord.

Star Throwing

At a seaside resort, depressed and unable to sleep, naturalist Loren Eiseley walked the beach for hours. He watched as local shell collectors picked up shells containing starfish, which would later be boiled out, dried in the sun and sold. He thought, yes, the strong exploit the weak.

One morning, just after dawn, he watched a lone figure picking up any living starfish he could find and hurling them back into the sea. Eiseley thought he was mad, but he came back the next morning and found the man doing the same thing. The man was there seven days a week, flinging stranded starfish into the sea. He fascinated the naturalist, who viewed him as a symbol of hope in a despairing world. Eiseley found his own spirits restored.

The starfish thrower affirmed life in the face of overwhelming odds. Open your eyes for an opportunity to affirm hopefulness and life today.

Hope in the Lord! For with the Lord there is steadfast love, and...great power to redeem. (Psalm 130:7)

Father, what can we do to make the world a better place?

Kids Being Kids Again

Perhaps the worst event that can befall a youngster is the death of a loved one. At Camp Comfort in Goochland, Virginia, bereaved children are not only helped to confront their emotions; they can learn to be kids again.

Camp founder Lynne Hughes, who lost both of her parents before she was 12, wants to help children deal with the grief they're experiencing. The campers spend time just being children and having fun, but they also focus on activities that help them confront their feelings of loss. In one ritual, they write notes to departed loved ones, attach them to balloons and fling them skyward. "Dear Mom," read one, "Have you met God yet?"

Hughes' husband, Kelly, now understands the magic of the camp. When their son Evan was born, Kelly realized that "I may not be there for Evan one day. I knew Camp Comfort was exactly what we should be doing."

Give consolation to God's wounded children.

Comfort, O comfort My people, says your God. (Isaiah 40:1)

Comforter, guide me to find the right path.

Creating Better Everydays

Amidst the daily hustle and bustle, it's easy to lose sight of simple, creative ways we can enhance our lives. Here are reminders and suggestions for living life creatively, peacefully:

- Meaning lies in relationships, not in words.
- Let yourself be influenced for good, then influence others.
- Respect is the attempt to understand.
- Believe in unrealized potential.
- Never hurry.
- Win by letting go.
- Live, love, laugh and learn.
- Take 100 percent responsibility and 0 percent control.
- Optimism is the biology of hope.
- Show up, be generous.

Finally, remember that life is not a spectator sport. Take an active role in your own.

The fear of the Lord is life indeed; filled with it one rests secure and suffers no harm. (Proverbs 19:23)

Creator, I will keep in mind that nothing is ever as it seems.

The British are Coming...On Bicycles!

Joe McCarthy usually produces films for corporate clients. But after reading an account of the American Revolution's Battle of Brooklyn, he raised $100,000 to make a film about it.

While he might have preferred hiring 35,000 red-coated extras, he settled for a fleet of red cars and teenagers wearing red t-shirts on bicycles to represent the British. A single actor took on the roles of Lord Stirling and a modern-day tour guide/narrator.

Lacking a big budget, McCarthy dispensed with sets. Whenever possible, he shot on the exact location the events happened, choosing to let the irony of skyscrapers and pavement play a role in "The Brave Man."

By the way, the British won the battle. But the fighting gave George Washington and his troops time to escape to Manhattan and the chance to fight again another day.

Remember that the future has its roots in the past.

Good things and bad, life and death, poverty and wealth, come from the Lord. (Sirach 11:14)

Lord, show us how to follow our dreams.

Choose Role Models with Care

Not all sports figures want to be role models to their young fans. Nevertheless, they are.

A lot of people look up to professional basketball player Marcus Camby, literally, since the center is 6-foot-11. And he seems to feel a commitment to them, especially children.

An education major in college, Camby started the "March With Marcus" program a few years ago designed to promote the value of education and improve student attendance in poor districts in New York City. He provides supplies and visits when he can.

The athlete still hopes to become a school principal one day and is taking courses on-line during the summers.

"In my old high school in Hartford, there was this vice principal, Frank DeLoreto, and I always wanted to be like him."

The best role models have heroes of their own.

Let us set an example. (Judith 8:24)

It takes much strength of character and soul to be an example of Godly living, Father. Please give me Your strength.

Turning Off the Tube

Fact: The average child watches 1,180 minutes of TV a week–and has 38.5 minutes a week of meaningful conversation with his or her parents.

Fact: An average child spends 900 hours a year in school–but more than 1,000 hours a year in front of the television set.

It sounds like time to turn off the tube.

Gary Legwold and his son, Ben, did just that. In fact Ben had an assignment from his English teacher to stop viewing for seven days and write about that week without television.

"We made it through–and even enjoyed it," says Legwold. "Ben and I went to one basketball playoff game and listened to others on the radio. We went to movies, visited friends, and lingered over meals and piano lessons. There seemed to be more time–and more peace–in the house."

Good things happen when you tune in to your loved ones.

Pleasant words are like a honeycomb, sweetness to the soul and health to the body. (Proverbs 16:24)

Help me find You, Lord, in the silence of this day, as well as in its confusion.

Creating Happy Campers

On the lawn of New Hope Baptist Church in Hackensack, New Jersey, five and six-year-old campers gather around a pair of basketballs and a hoop while Camp New Hope director Moses Whitaker looks on in amusement. "We don't really care who wins or loses," he says. "But they do."

The aim of the two-week-long day camp is to offer children recreational and outdoor options. Most of the children who attend are black, but there are Hispanic and white youngsters as well.

Whitaker says he simply wants to provide a fun, healthy outlet for children who need it most. "At least for two weeks, they can say they had a good time. And their good time gives them a chance to bond with children of different ethnic backgrounds."

Our hope for the next generation of adults comes from all who reach out to today's children.

Have we not all one father? Has not one God created us? Why then are we faithless to one another? (Malachi 2:10)

I harbor hope that we all learn to live together, Lord.

Lighten Up!

Have you found yourself just going through the motions of life recently? Getting to work, doing errands, making sure the dog is fed, but not really enjoying any of it?

Author Christina Boyle Cush came up with a list of 101 ways to have fun in the summer, but most can be experienced any time of the year. Try some of her suggestions, or use this list as inspiration:

- Serve s'mores for dessert.
- Rent a bicycle built for two.
- Use purple ink.
- Do something active you haven't tried in at least 15 years.
- Put out a bowl of fruit or candy at work and make instant friends.
- Eat dinner by candlelight.
- Pick four spots to visit before the summer ends.

Incorporate fun into your life: Life's too short not to.

Rejoice always. (1 Thessalonians 5:16)

Fill us with ideas to truly celebrate the gift of life, Lord.

So Many Reasons to Celebrate

The Long Island community of Riverhead has long had authentic Polish bakeries and craft shops. Even the art on the street signs is done in red and white with the Polish Eagle emblem. In 1975 the local civic organization was looking for an event to raise funds. They had no idea their plans would give birth to an annual tradition.

Now Polish Town is an annual street fair that hosts more than 150,000 visitors.

What's the special draw? The old-fashioned wedding held at St. Isidore's Church. The centerpiece of the town and the fair, St. Isidore's goes all out to take guests back in time with authentic costumes, rites and music. "For those few hours, everyone on Pulaski Street is Polish," says regular attendee Mary Haschak.

Work to develop your community's spirit.

Have unity of spirit, sympathy, love for one another, a tender heart, and a humble mind. (1 Peter 3:8)

Remind us, Creator of all, that our unique histories can be planks in a bridge, as opposed to bricks in a wall.

Volunteering for Vacation

Nathan Smith, 15, wanted to check out all the rides at amusement parks. Instead, he, his parents and siblings spent their time off doing labor for the poor. They volunteered for vacation.

More and more families are skipping the usual vacation activities to help others. For the Smiths, this meant refurbishing the homes of the elderly or disabled poor in Tumacacori, Arizona. One was 85-year-old Hermenia Lopez whose eyes filled with tears when she saw how this family made her home livable.

"I've always felt that those of us who have comfortable lives have an obligation to help those who are less fortunate," says Richard Smith. His wife, Debbie, adds: "Our children learned that any life worth living involves giving to others."

"It wasn't what I wanted," Nathan says, "but it made me feel I was needed and could make a difference in someone's life."

What you want and what you need may not be the same.

Help the poor for the commandment's sake and in their need do not send them away empty-handed. (Sirach 29:9)

In You, Master, I find rest; refresh my soul.

Urban Naturist

American artist Rockwell Kent was raised in a prominent and wealthy family. But it was the raw, rugged, untamed beauty of nature which inspired him to paint.

For Kent, the outdoors fueled his passion for painting. Although he had studied architecture and had illustrated many books, painting remained his true love. His work includes luminous landscapes, graphics, advertising art and other types of expression, illustrating his ability to use his talent in many forms.

Your God-given interests can be used in a multitude of ways to serve others, as well as for self-fulfillment. Think about it, the possibilities are limitless: if you like sports, you might coach a local team; if you enjoy reading, you could teach literacy.

Put your gifts to work for the world and yourself.

Those who love God must love their brothers and sisters. (1 John 4:21)

Remind us that we have a bounty of gifts from You, Lord, with which to serve others.

Help from the Past

When the John J. Harvey, a steam-powered fireboat, was first introduced in the 1930s, it was considered one of the most powerful fire-fighting vessels of its time.

That perception was extremely accurate. Seventy years later, when the Twin Towers of New York City's World Trade Center collapsed after the terrorist attack of September 11, 2001, a volunteer crew fired up the John J. Harvey since none of the hydrants west of the World Trade Center worked.

Despite the fact that it had been de-commissioned due to budget cuts, the ship pulled through, pumping Hudson River water through its hoses and onto the inferno.

Often, help arrives from the most unlikely of places and people. When have you recently offered a helping hand to a friend, family member or co-worker? Your offer could be a vital sign of hope.

Let love be genuine...love one another with mutual affection. (Romans 12:9,10)

Jesus, help me focus on others' needs by following Your example.

Of Lemonade and Shady Trees

Maybe it's because of her name, but Nancy Beach readily admits that summer is her favorite season.

"But if you're not careful," she warns, "you can miss out on the 'summers' of the soul." Beach is referring to those times when life is abundant and good. She recommends incorporating activities into life in order to savor more fully the joy life offers.

First, put a healthy emphasis on recreation. Beach believes the challenge is to find activities which truly refresh and restore your spirit.

Next, make time for celebration. She points out that a thread of celebration is woven into the pages of the Bible, and that feasting, music, and dancing were always important.

Finally, put on an attitude of gratitude. Beach quotes Lewis Smedes who notes that when we say "thank You" to God, we complete the gift-giving experience.

With gratitude in your hearts sing psalms, hymns, and spiritual songs to God. (Colossians 3:16)

Thank You, Heavenly Father, for seasons of both earth and heart.

True Friendship

During National Friendship Week, a message making the rounds in cyberspace highlighted some of the joys of friendship and offered tips for those who would be friends. See if you agree—and what you might add.

"Learn from the mistakes of others. You can't live long enough to make them all yourself."

"Anger is only one letter short of danger."

"Great minds discuss ideas; average minds discuss events; small minds discuss people."

"Friends, you and me...you brought another friend...and then there were three...we started our group...our circle of friends...there is no beginning or end..."

"Yesterday is history. Tomorrow is mystery. Today is a gift."

If you have a friend you've been meaning to call, do it now.

One who forgives an affront fosters friendship, but one who dwells on disputes will alienate a friend. (Proverbs 17:9)

Lord, may we befriend the friendless and thereby share with all the joy of true friendship.

Inspired by a Visionary

Walt Disney was not only a visionary; he used his vision as a motivating tool.

As the story goes, when the original Disneyland in Anaheim, California, was being designed and constructed, all the parties involved agreed that a specific system and timetable was necessary to keep costs under control and ensure that the park opened on time. That meant that Sleeping Beauty Castle, which was to be visible from anywhere in the park, was to be built last.

Not so, insisted Disney, who wanted the castle built first, believing it would provide a vision for the rest of the construction. Its image would remind workers on a daily basis what the park was meant to be, and motivate them to make it happen. The result is a tribute to the human imagination.

Take time out each day to let ourselves imagine what we can make happen in our lives. And then, go to work.

Happy is the person who meditates on wisdom and reasons intelligently, who reflects...on her ways and ponders her secrets. (Sirach 14:20-21)

I will employ my vision in hopes of betterment, Spirit.

History Shouldn't be a Mystery

You might think that naming the sides which fought the Civil War is a "no brainer," but 24 percent of American teens could not answer: North and South.

A national survey sponsored by the Colonial Williamsburg Foundation asked 1000 young people basic history questions. The results won't warm the hearts of educators or parents. 17 percent didn't know that there were thirteen original colonies; 19 percent weren't aware that the three branches of government are the legislative, executive and judicial; and 31 percent couldn't name Francis Scott Key as the author of "The Star-Spangled Banner."

Students have a responsibility to learn. But parents, teachers, school administrators, government officials, in fact all adults have obligations, too. We need to provide the means for all youngsters to get a quality education for the sake of their future and that of our country and world. That's really a "no brainer."

Give me understanding so that I may know your decrees. ...that I may live. (Psalm 119:125, 144)

Spirit of Knowledge, dwell within our minds and hearts. Grant us Your grace this day to grow in understanding.

The Catcher and the Cell Phone

Everyone complains about cell phones, but does anyone do anything about them?

Well, what one professional baseball player did about one cell phone amazed a Long Island couple.

Elizabeth and Marty, who had been at Yankee Stadium watching their team defeat the Kansas City Royals, returned home and realized they'd lost their cell phone at the ballpark.

They didn't expect to get it back but were pleasantly surprised when Hector Ortiz, the Royal's catcher, called them.

"He had bought the seats behind us for a group of kids and after the game he went up to talk to his guests. He spotted the phone," notes Elizabeth, "and took the time and effort to call us."

This is one cell phone story without any complaints.

There's always time for kindness and courtesy.

Pay...respect to whom respect is due, honor to whom honor is due. (Romans 13:7)

Encourage me, Jesus, to take a little time every day to do something that will help family, friends, and strangers.

Banned Words

Editors at most national magazines, wordsmiths at heart, have quirky pet peeves when it comes to language.

David Granger of *Esquire* doesn't like the word "some," as in the sentence: 'Some 700,000 readers buy the men's magazine.'"

"People use it to mean 'approximately,'" Granger told *The New York Times,* "and it just has no meaning. I've tried to come to terms with it, but it makes my skin crawl."

Other editors have banned words and phrases including "bad hair day," "genius," "essential" and "edgy."

It's fun to romp through the reasons certain words bug certain editors. It's also a good excuse to evaluate your own usage.

How is your language, written and spoken? Does it reflect the genuine you? Is it intelligent? Respectful? Consider your words' effect before choosing hurtful or offensive language.

Pleasant speech multiplies friends, and a gracious tongue multiplies courtesies. (Sirach 6:5)

Increase my awareness, Lord, of how my words affect my world.

The Nation's Oldest Employee

"I've lived in three centuries," says Robert Eisenberg, then 103, in a 2001 *People* magazine article. "It's really hard to believe." The centenarian continues to work every day. Retirement is a dirty word to this vibrant senior.

The overseer of zipper production at Zabin Industries Inc., a company he owned for many years, he is very possibly the oldest employee in the country. The present owner raves, "he's got remarkable mental abilities...I find myself forgetting his age."

Eisenberg does not subscribe to any special diet or regimen. He eats "anything and everything... (and) enjoy(s) white wine." Though he retired at age 72 for about ten years, he returned to work because he got bored.

Service and usefulness as well as moderation may or may not be keys to longevity, but they certainly make our time worthwhile.

How attractive is sound judgment in the gray-haired, and for the aged to possess good counsel! (Sirach 25:4)

Lord, I will realize the virtues of hard work.

Thirst Quenchers

"Whether it's because of an overwhelming to do list or challenging circumstances, we all go through times when God seems far away," says an article in *Today's Christian Woman*. The magazine offered suggestions from several readers:

- Sharron McDonald of Arkansas says she thumbs through old journal entries, which "help me remember how many times God has shown me His love."

- Dawn Pitsch of Washington finds that "when I talk to a friend who hasn't experienced God's love and forgiveness, I'm reminded of all I have in Christ," she observes.

- Kristen Szweda of Wisconsin "placed a Bible where I could see it during the day to serve as a visible reminder of God's promise to never leave or forsake me. I'm thankful He's there to walk with me through the joys of life, as well as the struggles."

God never leaves us. Just open your heart.

Abide in Me as I abide in you. (John 15:4)

Accept my gratitude, Lord, no matter how intangible Your presence may seem at times.

Creating Satisfied Employees

It really doesn't take much to turn a disgruntled worker into a satisfied employee, one who feels his or her job is important. All that's required, in many cases, is a boss who recognizes problems. By giving more attention and credit where it's due, a troublesome situation can be turned around.

Here are some suggestions for making employees feel their work is worthwhile:

- Talk to them frequently.
- Listen to their opinions.
- Explain the importance of doing the job well.
- Watch for special abilities and praise good work.
- Ask for workers' input on various problems.

Simply put, we all want to feel that what we do daily has meaning and importance. Help others uncover their significance.

I have set you an example. (John 13:15)

Help me inspire others to work to the best of their ability, Carpenter of Nazareth.

Hope Truck

Joshua Glick was in Manhattan on September 11, 2001, brought there by his job with an indoor landscaping company.

In fact, he was supposed to be within blocks of the World Trade Center, but he and his partner had gotten a late start. His company dispatcher ordered the pair out of the city after news of the terrorist attack, but Joshua had one more unscheduled stop – his stepmother's office.

Not only did Joshua take his stepmother home, but five others from her midtown office – and about 40 more who hopped on board his truck for stretches as it traveled north; a mix of people from various professions, races and nationalities, making the journey together, seated side-by-side on bags of soil and surrounded by potted plants.

They were a group of people united in sorrow and hope – and by the actions of one very thoughtful young man.

Love one another with mutual affection. (Romans 12:10)

In my darkest hour, Father, I look to You, and I find hope and comfort and peace.

Dilbert-like Management

The popular syndicated cartoon, *Dilbert,* is required humor therapy for millions. In today's workplace many must endure *Dilbert*-like illogical managers.

In a "*Dilbert* Quotes" contest a while ago, people submitted quotes from their *Dilbert*-like managers. Here are a few doozies:

- "As of tomorrow, employees will only be able to access the building using individual security cards. Pictures will be taken next Wednesday and employees will receive their cards in two weeks."

- I need "a list of specific unknown problems we will encounter."

- "Communication is a problem, but the company is not going to discuss it with the employees."

- "Teamwork is...people doing what I say."

We live and work under absurd even wacky circumstances. Laugh at them. That will help you through the day.

Our mouth was filled with laughter, and our tongue with shouts of joy. (Psalm 126:2)

Thanks for the ability to laugh at life, God.

Your Kind of Music

Do you play your musical instrument at home, but really want to join a band and get on stage? Here's what a group of amateur musicians and nightclub owners suggest:

Check out the local music store. Most music stores have a bulletin board with various music business postings like the best place to find a music teacher, "round robin" folk sessions at people's homes, and groups looking for players of certain kinds of instruments and those interested in specific genres.

Sign up for a workshop or music festival. You're sure to find opportunities there. Wear something—a T-shirt or a pin—that says something about the instrument you play and your tastes.

Find open-mike nights. Many clubs feature these opportunities for amateur musicians, which are usually listed in the entertainment section of newspapers.

Don't be afraid to enjoy and share your talents with others.

Praise Him with trumpet...lute and harp... tambourine and dance...strings and pipe! Praise Him with clanging cymbals. (Psalm 150:3,4-5)

Thank You, Creator, for the gift of music and song.

Major League Gumption

He was only six when his right arm was mangled by a truck and had to be amputated. But Peter Wyshner, later known as Pete Gray, was determined to leave the Pennsylvania coalfields to play professional baseball.

Creating techniques to field and bat one-handed, he spent several years in the minors before signing with the St. Louis Browns in 1945. Gray clobbered fastballs with his hefty bat, but couldn't handle offspeed pitches and, with the return of players at the end of World War II, he was out of the majors.

Going back home, he regularly visited hospitals to encourage wartime amputees. He also faced his own demons as he struggled with alcohol. In his eighties, Pete Gray was asked about what he was most proud. His answer: "I never gave up."

We don't control everything that happens in our lives. We do get to choose how we regard ourselves and use our abilities.

While we still were sinners Christ died for us. ...Now...will we be saved through Him. (Romans 5:8,9)

Spirit of Courage, sometimes I just want to take the easy way. Show me, instead, Your way.

Bringing it Together

In 1990 Carol Ann Bonds became principal of the Holland, Texas, Elementary School. Soon she found she was much more than that. Paying special attention to students who felt ill, she would often drive them to a nearby hospital. Knowing that many households were without health insurance, she would convince the hospital to overlook expenses.

But Bonds wanted a real solution. So she applied for and received a grant from the state government and opened several school-based clinics that serve area residents. Volunteer doctors staff them and visits never cost more than ten dollars. Those who can't pay can work off their fee in community service.

Various elements are often available to help solve a problem, but someone is needed to organize them. Ms. Bonds says, "If one person brings together other thoughtful, committed people, it's incredible what can take place."

Are you that thoughtful, committed person?

Good works are conspicuous. (1 Timothy 5:25)

Here I am, Lord. Guide me to do Your will.

Rocky Mountain High

"There was no guardrail. Five feet below, sharp gray boulders caught at the swiftly flowing current. A fall would be disastrous," says Nicole Phinney, as she recounts making her way across a 10-foot bridge of Aspen logs. "My heart was in my throat by the time I stepped onto the far bank."

Phinney, an experienced hiker, conquered her fear. Now she turned to the four middle-aged women, including her mom, who were trekking through the Colorado Rockies under her leadership. One by one they successfully crossed the bridge. Over the next five days, these gutsy women bonded together in faith as they tackled more obstacles than they'd ever imagined.

"We saw the impossible become possible," says Phinney. "God's love for us was demonstrated not only through nature, but also in our love for each other."

Welcome God's presence and His many gifts to us.

Those who love Me will keep My word, and My Father will love them, and We will come to them and make Our home with them. (John 14:23)

Open our hearts to new ways of knowing You, Loving God.

Unlocking the Secrets of Success

When Esmeralda Santiago came to the United States at the age of 13, school administrators placed her in a class for "slow" learners, since she could not speak English. Determined to prove herself, she even studied picture books meant for young children to master the language of her new country.

Now a magna cum laude graduate of Harvard, she has become a respected author embracing both her Puerto Rican and American heritage. Santiago believes the keys to the adjustment of any immigrant are hard work, a sense of pride and dignity, openness to the new culture and determination not to be limited by the low expectations of others. Her credo applies to anyone who seeks a successful, satisfying life.

Live up to the best, not the worst; the highest, not the lowest that is in you.

The wisdom of the scribe depends on the opportunity of leisure. (Sirach 38:24)

Infuse my spirit with passion, Divine Master. Help me live out my fullest potential.

The Problem of Evil

After the horror of September 11, 2001, when hijacked passenger airplanes were crashed into the World Trade Center, the Pentagon and a field in Pennsylvania, many people, including clergy, tried to make sense of it.

"We will seek justice...in which hatred and desires for revenge must never have a part," said New York's Cardinal Edward Egan.

In San Francisco, the Very Rev. Alan Jones of Grace Episcopal Cathedral, believed "We can choose... despair and resentment and...vengeance, or we can...work for....God's peace...wholeness and integrity, justice and mercy."

"God stands with us, weeps with us, strengthens us, mourns with us," noted Rev. Rick Boyer, of Maplewood, New Jersey's Prospect Presbyterian Church.

The Rev. Samuel Johnson Howard, Vicar of Trinity Church, Wall Street, said that "God's anger in the face of evil will be known in love, in compassion, in mercy. ...Only God's justice is perfect justice."

Hold fast to love and justice and wait continually for your God. (Hosea 12:6)

God, give us peace!

The Sounds of Silence

Collegian Brett Banfe believes that we should listen twice as much as we talk.

The New Jerseyian vowed silence for an entire year. Why exactly would he want to mute himself? In an e-mail interview, he suggested it had to do with promoting self-discipline in himself and others. "It's mainly about commitment," he wrote. "Besides, no one else, except monks, has tried to do this."

He achieved his aim and Congress even gave him a commendation for "inspiring others to meet their goals."

We have two ears but only one mouth. Perhaps we should all listen twice as much as we speak. But only if we genuinely, truly, honestly listen.

For everything there is a season, and a time for every matter under heaven...a time to keep silence, and a time to speak. (Ecclesiastes 3:1,7)

Holy Spirit, open my ears, my heart, my eyes to the people and events around me.

On Success and Leadership

Here are thoughts on leadership from Brian Tracy, author of *The 100 Absolutely Unbreakable Laws of Business Success*.

- Be honest with every person.
- Make decisions even in adversity.
- Respond to the world as it is, not as you'd like it to be.
- Use power wisely; you'll be given more.
- Have a clear vision of the future and realize it.
- Radiate confidence.
- Be empathetic.
- Be resilient.
- Know what you believe in; think for yourself.
- Keep calm.
- Aim for the ideal and for continuous improvement.
- Anticipate the future; expect the unexpected.

A real leader serves others.

To each is given a manifestation of the Spirit for the common good. (1 Corinthians 12:7)

Give me the courage, Jesus, to be successful where I am.

Courage, On the Bike and Off

There are few tales of courage and determination as riveting as the one told by Lance Armstrong in his book *It's Not About the Bike*.

Several years ago, Armstrong, a top bicyclist, was found to have advanced testicular cancer. The cancer, though eminently curable in its early stages, had progressed and had spread throughout his body. Doctors told him he had at best a 50-50 chance of survival. Later one doctor confessed he thought Armstrong's odds were far worse. But Armstrong beat the odds, facing cancer with grit and the love and support of family and friends.

Most corporate sponsors for the Tour De France abandoned him after he lost all of his muscle mass to chemotherapy and they have regretted it ever since.

Today, Armstrong is happily married, a proud father and, as a two-time winner of bicycling's Tour De France, at the very top of his sport.

Never give up hope, whatever the odds.

The Lord created medicines out of the earth, and the sensible will not despise them. (Sirach 38:4)

Divine Physician, give the sick victory over their ills.

Visualization May Hold the Answer

The great geneticist of maize (corn), Barbara McClintock, was so intelligent her ability to solve complex problems of corn genetics made her appear supernatural. But McClintock attributes her success to intuition and subconscious revelations.

"I cannot tell necessarily where they come from, but the whole thing is solved suddenly," says McClintock about her moments of epiphany.

This type of experience has happened to other geniuses, most often mathematicians and physicists. Albert Einstein, for example, worked on problems by playing with, as he put it, "certain signs and more or less clear images which can be voluntarily reproduced and combined." Einstein said that he reached his theory of relativity by imagining he was riding a light wave, and then looking around and describing what he saw.

Stuck on a problem? Try visualizing the answer and rely on your intuition. That may be where the solution lies.

**Give me now wisdom and knowledge.
(2 Chronicles 1:10)**

Holy Spirit, I am grateful for my instincts and feelings, as well as my intellect. May I use them wisely.

A Gentle Reminder

"Make your bed! Pick up your socks! Clean the closet! These are words just about all parents have barked out time and again," says Annette Miller. "But," she asks, "is the yelling really worth it?"

According to Miller's article in *Newsweek*, messy rooms have become the top issue between parents and middle school students. The current thinking is that parents should try to help their kids tackle the mess, fully aware that no amount of yelling will ever "turn a slob into a neatnik."

This lesson applies to other relationships. Sometimes we harp on the same issues with the same people. What makes us think we will suddenly inspire different behavior?

Resolve to approach an ongoing issue with a friend, a co-worker or family member from a gentler and more helpful perspective.

A soft answer turns away wrath, but a harsh word stirs up anger. (Proverbs 15:1)

Lord, direct my energy to useful purposes.

Life Lessons

Experience teaches us wonderful and valuable lessons. Here are a few that deserve to be shared:

- Never tell a child that his or her dreams are outlandish.
- Friends will hurt you once in a while. Forgive them.
- Sometimes you have to learn to forgive yourself first.
- No matter what happens to you, the world keeps turning.
- Credentials on a wall do not make you a decent person.
- There are many ways of falling and staying in love.
- Two people look at the same thing and see something totally different.
- When you think you have no more to give, you will find the strength to help a friend in need.

Life teaches that you never stop learning. Learn well for your sake and the world's.

Hear instruction and be wise, and do not neglect it. (Proverbs 8:33)

Holy Spirit, instruct us, enlighten us.

A September Surprise

On a summer day, Howard Forvour discovered that the 50 flags he had spaced neatly in the front yard of his Moorestown, New Jersey, home had been stolen. Forvour, a World War II Army engineer, was disappointed, but as he says, "I let it go. I thought I'd just replace the flags."

What a pleasant surprise it was for him when, on a late September day, he spotted a plastic bag on his lawn containing the stolen flags. Inside the bag was a note from the culprits. It read: "We all felt bad and completely regretted doing it. …We are truly sorry."

A forgiving sort, Forvour bears the thieves no ill will. He says, "I'd give them flags of their own to put on their lawn."

Apologies and forgiveness ruled the day. Let us strive for that outcome in our daily relationships.

Forgive, and you will be forgiven. (Luke 6:37)

Lord of forgiveness, help me to let go and love.

Promises Kept

When a federal judge said "I have never seen more egregious misconduct by the government," Elouise Cobell of the Blackfeet Indian tribe was finally vindicated.

It was a crowning moment in a decades-long endeavor to bring justice to a people whose rights had been violated. Through agreements reaching back as far as 1887, the American government was to have managed and distributed funds related to the sale and lease of reservation lands.

"I remembered as a little girl," Cobell told *Parade* magazine, "the elders would…wonder where the money was. But they didn't know what to ask. You felt so powerless." After earning a degree in accounting, Cobell began putting the puzzle together. Experts ultimately expect the government settlement to Native Americans to be in the $20 to $40 billion range.

Each of us needs to hold our government accountable for justice to ourselves and others. That's part of good citizenship.

Give justice to the weak and the orphan; maintain the right of the lowly and the destitute. (Psalm 82:3)

Do not let us grow weary, God, in our efforts for justice.

Unforgettable Gifts

Want to give your children gifts that won't be forgotten? Here are a few suggestions from writer and parent, Susan Alexander Yates. Give:

The gift of affection. Even if you didn't grow up in an emotionally expressive home, try to hug your children often and tell them that you love them. It may feel awkward at first, but soon it will feel right.

The gift of family traditions. Traditions can be a special family dinner once a week or bedtime rituals. They will help instill in your children a sense of stability and continuity.

The gift of laughter. Teach your child to laugh. Collect funny lists and read them aloud at dinner. Get a joke book. Cultivate friendships with people gifted in humor, but not sarcasm which appears funny but causes pain.

Encourage your children to be generous, giving people, too.

> **If you...know how to give good gifts to your children, how much more will your Father...give good things to those who ask Him!**
> **(Matthew 7:11)**

Help parents give children gifts that truly matter, Abba.

Good Judgment Saves the Day

San Jose State College student and aspiring actress Kelly Bennett dreamed of seeing her name in the headlines, but never thought she would. Then, during a normal evening's work at a local photo lab, her keen judgment helped prevent what could have become a Columbine High School-like incident.

Kelly, processing film that had been left the day before, saw images of guns and bombs. After showing the pictures to co-workers, she decided to call her San Jose police officer father.

When a local college student came to pick up the developed film he was arrested. It seems that the student "hated everybody" and had been making violent threats for months.

We never know when fate and circumstances may necessitate our taking immediate action. As for Kelly, her father said it best. "I'm not surprised by her response at all. Just proud."

Show good judgment. Use your head and your heart.

Keep alert, stand firm. (1 Corinthians 16:13)

Holy Spirit, make me alert and courageous.

The Legacy of a Violin

When Isaac Stern, the great violinist, died in New York City at age 81, he left more than 100 albums–and Carnegie Hall.

Born in 1920 in Ukraine, he came with his parents to the United States when he was ten-months-old, settling in San Francisco. Starting on the piano at 6, Stern, two years later, picked up a friend's violin–and the rest is musical history.

Mentor to such master musicians as Itzhak Perlman, Yo-Yo Ma and Pinchas Zukerman, Stern, at his peak, performed 200 concerts a year on his beloved 1700s Guarneri violin.

Then in 1960, Stern rallied fellow artists and influential New Yorkers to stop a developer from razing Carnegie Hall. Succeeding at the task, Stern later said: "I knew that this building could not disappear from the face of the earth."

Before you die, do all you can to make life sound a little sweeter for those you leave behind.

Have regard for your name, since it will outlive you. ...The days of a good life are numbered, but a good name lasts forever. (Sirach 41:12,13)

A song of praise I send to You, Creator, for You have blessed the work of our hands.

Coping with Conflict

Conflict is a stressful yet integral part of life. The key isn't in trying to eliminate it but rather in learning to handle it wisely.

Seattle's Hope Heart Institute offers these dos and don'ts:

- Don't try to avoid conflict. It'll be internalized and eat "you up inside." When current problems aren't talked over, future conflicts are more likely.
- Don't try to dominate others or bully them into submitting to your point of view.
- Don't be self-centered. Others have legitimate interests as well.
- Do present your side of the story.
- Do listen carefully to the other person's side.
- Do suggest compromises if possible.

We can't end stress. However, we can keep it in check.

Some people keep silent because they have nothing to say, while others keep silent because they know when to speak. (Sirach 20:6)

Jesus, make us bearers of peace with justice and respect.

Hi, New Moms and Dads

It's impossible to fully grasp the permanent responsibilities of parenthood until the baby arrives. While the joy more than compensates for the demands, even thoughtful couples can become overwhelmed with balancing work against the needs of a little one.

Writer Jane A. G. Kise poses a thought-provoking question for those who feel caught in this situation: "What does it mean to stay at home?" She suggests evaluating options including part-time day care, working evenings or juggling schedules with a spouse. Kise also recommends expanding your support network.

"The security that comes from finding church groups or other networks smoothes abrupt changes," she says.

Perhaps a fresh look at an ongoing struggle in your life will bring forth a new solution. And don't worry about asking for help.

Be at peace among yourselves.
(1 Thessalonians 5:13)

Creator God, show us the way to peace.

The Diderot Effect

When 18th-century philosopher Denis Diderot received a beautiful scarlet bathrobe, he wasted no time ridding himself of his old one. Little did he know the effect.

Diderot's essay, *Regrets on Parting with My Old Dressing Gown,* gives us an interesting take on simplicity.

"He grew dissatisfied with his study, with its threadbare tapestry, the desk, his chairs, and even the room's bookshelves," writes economist Juliet Schor. Little by little, he replaced each item with more elegant versions.

"In the end, Diderot found himself seated uncomfortably in the stylish formality of his new surroundings," says Schor. She calls it the "Diderot effect."

How many of us have found ourselves wanting a new tie to go with that new shirt, a new purse to go with those new shoes, or even new carpet for the new house?

Take time to think before making purchases or any choices.

One's life does not consist in the abundance of possessions. (Luke 12:15)

Master of All, protect us from greed.

Don't Close My School

Aging urban school buildings are forcing communities to decide what to do with them. Landmark them? Or, replace them with modern, up-to-date facilities? Some officials believe it is too expensive to renovate these buildings. Others feel the structures are special and should be preserved.

A 12-year-old boy whose school, built in 1895, faced closing, said, "I feel bad. That school's like a second home to me; the teachers are fine, and the principal is, too. I don't know why they're going to take it away."

Architectural historian Richard Longstreth says the schools are "visual and psychological cornerstones of the community. Built with bricks and steel and terra cotta, these are civic statements sited deliberately to be focal points and local landmarks."

What are the focal points and landmarks in your life?

**Godliness is valuable in every way...for both the present life and the life to come.
(1 Timothy 4:8)**

Teach us, Lord, what is truly valuable.

Prize-Winning Perspective

"Rarely have I felt such a failure of language," wrote Nobel Peace Prize winner Elie Wiesel after the terrorist attacks on America on September 11, 2001.

Eventually, says Wiesel, questions began to form. "Faced with such immense suffering, how can one go on working, studying, and simply living without sinking into despair? How is one to vanquish the fear?"

Wiesel believes hatred is at the root of evil everywhere.

"Racial hatred, ethnic hatred, political hatred, religious hatred. In its name," he claims, "it seems all is permitted."

But the world's response to the attacks form the basis of Wiesel's hope for the future. "This time, the terrorists failed," he observed. "They achieved the opposite of what they wanted. They moved people to transcend themselves and choose that which is noble in man."

Live a noble life.

Cease to do evil...seek justice, rescue the oppressed, defend the orphan, plead for the widow. (Isaiah 1:16-17)

Heal us, forgive us, strengthen us, O Merciful Lord.

Principles of Leadership

Secretary of State Colin Powell is a true American success story. A respected figure within the military, as well as in the political world, Powell believes that hard work and empathy are even more important than intelligence and self-fulfillment.

Over the years, Powell collected 13 rules that he wrote down and continues to live by. Here are a few that you might want to incorporate into your daily life:

- Get mad, then get over it.
- It can be done!
- Share credit.
- Remain calm and be kind.
- Be careful what you choose. You may get it.
- Have a vision. Be demanding.
- It ain't as bad as you think it is.

Consider the ethical standards that are important to you. Are you satisfied that you are living up to them?

Get wisdom. (Proverbs 4:5)

May I maintain my principles, Holy Spirit.

Café Mocha and Christianity

Pastors are now bringing church to coffee drinkers. At least that seems to be what's taking place in Munster, Indiana, where members of the Family Christian Center can now express their spiritual selves over a cup of java.

The church has opened a Starbucks in its lobby as part of its Heavenly Grounds Café & Bookstore, and Melodye and Steve Munsey, co-pastors of the Center, are happy with the results. "It tears down walls and the perception that church is stuffy and cold," says Rev. Melodye Munsey. "People can come in, relax and be with their friends in a wholesome and positive atmosphere."

Houston's Brentwood Baptist Church is opening a McDonald's jointly owned by the church and one of its members as part of its lifelong-learning center. Rev. Joe Samuel Ratliff says, "It's a holistic approach to reaching people."

You deserve a break today. Make it a prayerful respite.

They saw a charcoal fire there, with fish on it and bread...Jesus said to them, "Come and have breakfast." (John 21:9,12)

Thank You for Your sustenance, Risen Jesus.

Proud to Deliver

In the bustling metropolis of Mumbai or Bombay *dabbawalas* are essential.

Dabbawalas, or men who carry heavy loads of metal lunch pails, deliver meals (*dabbas*) from family kitchens to workplaces in the commercial center of Mumbai. Strict Indian dietary laws, as well as the pleasure of home-cooking, have made the system popular for over a century.

Supervisors plus 3000 deliverymen tote more than 100,000 lunches daily. *Dabbawalas* are proud of their reliability; lunches are rarely late or lost, and carriers are unfailingly punctual.

Trust and cooperation are essential to this system, but perhaps most important to the success of this complex network is the way *dabbawalas* are linked through kinship and religion.

Dedication and hard work still mean something. Pride and satisfaction in a job well done provides joy and sustenance.

Commit your work to the Lord. (Proverbs 16:3)

Help us do each day's work well, Carpenter of Nazareth.

A Taste of Normalcy

Jerry Korman and his wife, Mira Rivera, are convinced that some of the best work they've done raising their kids has come over plates of pasta.

"Family meals are a big deal to us," says Korman. "We've always seen them as a chance to relax and be together and talk about each other's day."

Psychologist Ron Taffel, author of *Nurturing Good Children Now*, says, "Dinnertime is one of the routines that kids absolutely need. It brings parents back into their lives concretely, just by sitting there."

Lynn Fredericks, mother of two sons, agrees: "When the world is a mess, if there's normalcy in the home–like sitting down to a meal–the kids feel there's a sense of security."

So tonight, pass the potatoes and the love.

Better is a dinner of vegetables where love is than a fatted ox and hatred with it.
(Proverbs 15:17)

Nourish me, Father. Fill me with Your life and love.

A Fire of Discovery

On an October night in 1987, an arsonist torched an old house in Lexington, Kentucky–and ignited a fire of architectural discovery that still smolders.

Scholars had once believed that Benjamin Henry Latrobe, America's first professional architect, designed the house at 326 Grosvenor Avenue, built in 1812. Born in England, Latrobe emigrated to the United States in 1796. He worked on the U.S. Capitol and the White House.

His connection with this Kentucky site was dismissed, however, and the building's importance diminished because of the difference between Latrobe's drawings and the actual house.

But on-site investigations after the fire at 326 Grosvenor Avenue confirmed the structure's fidelity to Latrobe's design and shed new light on a 19th-century architectural genius.

The truth isn't always obvious, but be willing to pursue it.

The promises of the Lord are promises that are pure, silver refined in a furnace...seven times. (Psalm 12:6)

Give me the wisdom, Father, to know Your will in the signs of the times.

Exercise Your Memory

None of us are immune from momentary memory lapses, those times when our memory fails us in everyday life. Here are a few ideas for exercising your memory and staying sharp:

- Having a routine for all the little everyday tasks makes it easy to retrace steps.
- Make a list of errands. Keep birthdays and important dates on a perpetual calendar. In other words, write things down!
- Repeat information such as names, telephone numbers and directions several times to yourself.
- Forget about multi-tasking. Focus on one task at a time.

In short, create routines that will help your memory function for you, not against you.

Memory is a marvelous gift. Yet, you're better off not dwelling on some things. If someone's hurt you, for your own sake, forgive. If you've hurt another, ask forgiveness.

Do this in remembrance of Me. (Luke 22:19)

I will not forget to talk with You today, Lord Jesus.

Domestic Tragedy, Global Support

When Geraldine Davie made a poster of her daughter Amy Davie O'Doherty after the destruction of the World Trade Center, she never imagined how far reaching its impact would be.

Amy Davie O'Doherty, an assistant broker at Cantor Fitzgerald, was missing. An Associated Press photographer took a picture of the poster and it appeared in many newspapers.

A few days later, Geraldine Davie got a call from a stranger in Washington. Other calls came from California, Texas, Hawaii, England, Switzerland and Brazil, too. "Have you found her?" they all asked. After hearing the answer, all offered condolences.

"People just wanted to say, 'I'm sorry,'" says Geraldine Davie. "It was nice to know that people around the world cared."

We are a global community. What affects one nation inevitably affects the world at large.

If one member suffers, all suffer...if one member is honored, all rejoice. (1 Corinthians 12:26)

Lord God, may the people of the world begin to find a common ground for peace.

The Garden of Angels

In 1997, Debi Faris buried an infant.

She also gave him a name, Michael. If she had done nothing, Michael would have been cremated, his remains put in a numbered box and the box filed away. Michael was an abandoned baby, one of scores left in public places each year in America. Debi Faris is simply a woman who heard about him and believed this anonymous baby boy deserved a proper burial.

Thus began the Garden of Angels in Calimesa, California. It is where Michael is buried, as well as Nathan, who was found in a trash bin, Dora, who washed up on a beach and dozens of others. Why did she do it? "They bring you a child wrapped in plastic and you look in their face."

Faris also became an advocate of preventative legislation, which offers legal protection to parents who abandon babies in safe places. All because one day she was moved to make a difference.

What moves you to make a difference for others?

Blessed are the merciful, for they will receive mercy. (Matthew 5:7)

Lord, grant me the wisdom to know my calling.

After Pain, Forgiveness

Wed in the 1960's, Karen Prowitz relished the prospect of moving into the first house she would share with her husband. As she emptied a dresser drawer, however, she discovered photos of her husband during his years of service in Korea.

To say she was shocked would be an understatement. Through the pictures Karen learned her husband had a son.

It was a painful journey, but she put her faith in God and forgave her husband. Sadly, the child's mother had moved and left no forwarding address. For 30 years, they prayed for the child, even as they raised their own three children.

Finally, Paul's now-grown son Sungwon Chi found them and the entire family rejoiced at the reunion.

Do you hold onto past hurts? Imagine how your life might be if you choose, instead, to let the healing power of God soothe your pain.

If you forgive others their trespasses, your heavenly Father will also forgive you. (Matthew 6:14)

Almighty God, help me reconcile with others.

Climb Every Mountain

Matt Bishopric, 14, reached the top of Mount Cardigan–in a wheelchair. The teen tackled the 3,121-foot high peak in Alexandria, Virginia, with help from classmates and volunteers. "It was good team work," he explains.

Matt, who has used a wheelchair since early childhood because of a spinal malformation, focuses always on what he can do–as opposed to what he can't, notes his teacher, Judy Wildman, who also made the climb. "He is just a remarkable kid," she offers. "He doesn't want anything special."

Matt credits his parents for his positive attitude. "They always told me I was just like everybody else and that if I try hard enough I can accomplish anything," he says. He hopes his actions deliver this message to all young people– indeed to all people: "They shouldn't let being in a wheelchair or anything else stop them from doing something they really want to do."

Trust God–and do all you can, all your days.

I am with you to save you and deliver you, says the Lord. (Jeremiah 15:20)

Merciful Lord, heal me when I am broken.

Relieving Stress

As we know from personal experience, life is full of stressful situations. Indeed, "I'm stressed out" has become part of our daily dialogue. Since we can't completely eliminate stress, the National Mental Health Association suggests ways to relieve it:

- *Talk it out.* Don't bottle up worries and concerns.

- *Escape for a while.* When things go wrong, escape from the problems for a time.

- *Do something for others.* Do something for somebody else instead of focusing on yourself and worrying all the time.

- *Take one thing at a time.* Focus on a few urgent tasks, do them one at a time, and set aside the rest.

- *Work off your anger.* Physical activity would be great.

Find ways to relieve the stresses in your life. Your heart, soul and mind will thank you.

Cast your burden on the Lord, and He will sustain you; He will never permit the righteous to be moved. (Psalm 55:22)

Strong Lord, shoulder my burdens with me. Without You I can not carry them.

In Vino Veritas

Tracy Cochran reluctantly accepted an invitation to travel to France with a group of wine journalists. The author of *Transformations: Awakening to the Sacred in Ourselves,* she told the journalists she knew next to nothing about wines but was hoping for a spiritual epiphany.

Cochran spent days sitting through lectures, field trips and wine tastings. Eventually she began to wonder if she had accepted the invitation under false pretenses.

Then one evening, she wandered into a vineyard and found the lesson for which she had been searching: "the gnarly vines were not rooted in soil, but in quartz stones and sandy red clay." The yield of vines raised in such difficult conditions is low, but the grapes have a full, clean, concentrated flavor. "The wines from these grapes have the potential for greatness," she observes.

The fortitude that comes with trials builds character in us.

Suffering produces endurance, and endurance produces character, and character produces hope, and hope does not disappoint us. (Romans 5:3-5)

Lord, abide with us through our trials.

Written on the Wall–and the Screen

When you next sit at a computer, think Zapf–Hermann Zapf, that is. Without him, the world would be without typefaces such as *Palatino* and *Optima*, *Zapf Dingbats* and *Zapf Chancery*.

In 1973, Zapf designed Marconi, the first font created for digital composition. "Designing metal type faces was done under the technical limitations of the casting process," he explains. "The digital technology of today gives you freedom which you never had in the time of hot metal."

But, Zapf doesn't use the computer for his craft. "I like to draw and use my hand," he says. Besides their place on the computer screen, Zapf's letters also appear in advertising, on cards and on the more than 58,000 names engraved in stone at the Vietnam Veterans Memorial in Washington, D.C.

The octogenarian designer's efforts seem "letter perfect."

Take care of details and the big matters won't be so hard.

The wisdom of the scribe depends on the opportunity of leisure. (Sirach 38:24)

In all I do this day, Father, may I reveal Your love.

Justice Is Served–with a Side of Coleslaw

In Kentucky's Jefferson County District Court, more than justice is served. Depending on the day, there might be homemade coleslaw, crab salad, fried chicken, or macaroni and cheese.

"Three kinds of cheese," notes Catherine Porter–"Miss Catherine" to all at the county's Hall of Justice. Each business day, judges, sheriff's deputies, city police, court bailiffs, clerks and administrators, even computer experts in town for a few weeks feast on the home cooking of this Paducah native. One judge ate only vegetarian and Porter made sure that's what she got.

The former owner of two restaurants now brings food from home in her car. "I don't have any kids, or nothing, and I just like to do for people," says Porter. "I just want to enjoy life with all those people. That's the reason I work every day; to be up there with all those people."

"Do for people"–a great idea for each of us.

**Love one another deeply from the heart.
(1 Peter 1:22)**

This day, Creator, may Your goodness and peace fill my heart, that I may know and do Your will.

Wealth—in the Eye of the Beholder

When a Spokane, Washington, parish youth group traveled to Mexico, the teens encountered something that shattered their perceptions of the poor. "We expected that because the people were poor, they would also be sad," a volunteer admits.

Yet, as the group dug trenches, constructed frames and poured foundations for homes in the impoverished community, they got to know many of the people. "We realized that though they were very poor, they were really very happy. They were...willing to give...whether it was a kind word or a tasty lunch, or even time with the small children," says another volunteer.

She added, "The mission helped us to see what Jesus was talking about when he said, 'Blessed are the poor.' We have so much more comfort and 'stuff'...but these poor of Mexico are rich in love and peace and faith."

What makes you rich in love, peace and faith?

Do not store up for yourselves treasures... where moth and rust consume...but store up for yourselves treasures in heaven. (Matthew 6:19,20)

Jesus, help us work to store up the riches of the spirit.

The Light of Kindness

Theresa Leone keeps a plastic cup as a reminder of a stranger's kind offer of water. Norma Hessic has the memory of a hand coming out of the darkness and pulling her to safety. Wheelchair-bound Tina Hansen is alive, thanks to two strangers, who carried her down 68 floors and out of the World Trade Center's north tower moments before it came crashing down.

Goodness shone throughout that terrible September 11 as demonstrated by every act of humanity by ordinary New Yorkers.

We all have things to be thankful for and carry reminders of good deeds done for us. Each of us has the ability to touch another person's life whether during the routine of daily life or in a time of crisis.

Ask yourself, how can I touch someone's life today?

Whoever gives even a cup of cold water...none of these will lose their reward. (Matthew 10:42)

May I seek not only to be comforted, Lord, but also to comfort.

Tips for Every Traveler

Travel writer Betsy Wade says some of the best advice she ever got was simple: read the fine print on everything. She has other useful tips to keep in mind as you plan your next vacation.

- If it matters to you: ask; that includes taxes, additional charges and type of bed and bathroom facilities.

- Don't pack anything you can't bear to lose–or to carry up a couple of flights of stairs.

- Take a map.

- There's no fast lane in a traffic jam or check-in line. Relax.

- Once in a while, let it enter your head that you just might be wrong.

The last point is worth remembering not only when you're on the road for business or pleasure, but as you are making your way through life. A little humility and patience can take you far.

The fruit of the Spirit is love, joy, peace, patience, kindness, generosity, faithfulness, gentleness and self-control. (Galatians 5:22-23)

Holy Family, guide me and guard me as I journey to new places in my life.

Young Scientists

Elite science students in high school don't just do projects for the Science Fair. They do science.

Take Alice Warren-Gregory. As a junior at Brooklyn's Midwood High School, she helped do brain research at Rockefeller University after school, under the guidance of a world-class neuroscientist. The then 17-year-old contributed to a scientific study as well as laying the groundwork for a promising future career.

Alice faced a lot of pressure in competing for the prestigious Intel Science Talent Search. Yet she found working toward a goal beneficial.

"I think it's really good to have something like Intel, because it gives you focus," said Alice. "I think some people in high school...get to their senior year and find that they've gotten caught up in trivial things. Right now is a really good time to work hard at something."

Good advice for scientists, non-scientists, teens and adults.

Strive for the greater gifts. (1 Corinthians 12:31)

Give us perseverance, Lord Christ.

Respect for All "Your Own"

He grew up in poverty, led a nomadic existence, worked as a writer and, after his immense popularity brought him wealth, became a philanthropist. James Michener had a gift for understanding diverse people and foreign places and encouraging his readers to appreciate them as well.

"I was born to a woman I never knew and raised by another who took in orphans," said Michener. "I do not know my background, my lineage, my biological or cultural heritage. But when I meet someone new, I treat them with respect. For after all, they could be my people."

He recognized the importance of empathizing with others however "different" they might be, saying, "When you're a writer, like me, you're not going to go very far unless you love people."

It's true for us all. If we don't love people, however far we may think we've gotten in life, we're just going around in circles.

Those who do not love a brother or sister whom they have seen, cannot love God whom they have not seen. (1 John 4:20)

I deserve to have every person I meet acknowledge my dignity, Holy God. And I owe the same to them.

A Life Story Worth Telling

It's impressive enough that Southern folk singer and songwriter Elizabeth "Libba" Cotton had her signature song, "Freight Train," recorded by some of the most famous pop and folk acts of the 1960s.

But what makes Libba Cotton's story all the more unusual is that she had written the song 50 years earlier, in 1904 when she was just 11-years-old.

What's more, she had taught herself how to play guitar, wrote what many consider classic folk songs, and sang into her 90s. Although she was left-handed, learning on a right-handed instrument didn't daunt her. She simply taught herself to finger the instrument upside down.

People with exceptional life stories inspire all of us to do great things. How have you tapped your potential lately? Consider the possibilities!

The gifts He gave were...for building up the body of Christ...to the measure of the full stature of Christ. (Ephesians 4:11,12,13)

Alert me to my potential, Holy Wisdom. Help me use my talents for God's glory, others' welfare and my own good.

One Big Thing

Many things can serve as inspiration. For the seventh century Greek poet, Archilochus, the hedgehog proved a muse and prompted him to make this observation: "The fox knows many things, but the hedgehog knows one big thing."

What "big thing" does the hedgehog know? It's this: No animal, no matter how big, ferocious or clever wants to eat a prickly, unappetizing ball.

When a hedgehog is in danger, special muscles allow it to curl up, covering its head and legs under a fleshy hood and bristling a thicket of spines on its back, frustrating predators. This has allowed the hedgehog to survive for almost 70 million years.

Today, the hedgehog is championed in the pages of children's books and ranges from Beatrix Potter's Mrs. Tiggy-Winkle to the recent video game incarnation, Sonic.

What "big thing" is most important to you?

From the fig tree learn its lesson: as soon as its branch becomes tender and puts forth its leaves, you know that summer is near. (Matthew 24:32)

Enlighten us, Holy Spirit.

And on the Seventh Day

If you ever find yourself next to Phil Callaway while you're waiting in line or flying on an airplane, he's likely to ask you his favorite question. Over the years he has collected hundreds of answers to his inquiry, "What has made your life rich?"

One person told him he had recently rediscovered the Sabbath. "Now, instead of shopping or fixing the car, our family attends an early church service and then spends the day together.

"We have hiked into the mountains, singing at the top of our lungs. We have serenaded the...old folks' homes. And we have sat under pine trees, reading the classics together."

The richness of this commitment lasts into the week. According to Callaway, the man observed, "We are better prepared for Monday because of Sunday."

Look at how you spend your Sundays–and your Mondays.

Refrain from trampling the Sabbath, from pursuing your own interests...call the Sabbath a delight...honorable. (Isaiah 58:13)

Open our hearts to Your call to a Sabbath rest, Lord.

Keeping Strong Bones

Although it's easy enough to take our bones for granted, keeping them strong is important.

"For at least half of women and one in eight men, bones are not bearing up as well as they should to sustain an active, independent old age free of debilitating fractures," according to *The New York Times* health columnist Jane Brody. As more of us live into our 70s, 80's and older, osteoporosis (bones seriously weakened by mineral loss) is becoming a common concern.

"Vertebral fractures result in lost height, a bent-over posture and often, chronic and debilitating pain," writes Brody. "Of those who break their hips, often in minor falls, half will never walk independently again and a quarter will die of complications within a year." Weight-bearing exercises, Vitamin D and a calcium-rich diet beginning in youth can help keep bones strong.

Our bodies are gifts from God. May we have the wisdom to keep them in as good repair as possible throughout life.

The Lord God formed man from the dust of the ground, and breathed into his nostrils the breath of life. (Genesis 2:7)

Jesus, help us maintain a healthy mind, body and spirit.

Role Modeling

"Kids will listen to what I say because I'm a football player," says NY Giants running back Tiki Barber. "I want to make sure I'm giving them the right message."

Nevertheless, Barber is the first to say that parents have more influence than they realize on their children's decisions. Here are four ways you can form a good game plan for parenting:

- Know what your kids are doing in and out of school and watch for behavioral changes.
- Set clear rules. Make consequences clear when those rules are broken.
- Stay involved in your kids' lives and activities. Praise and reward good behavior.
- Show your children you'll be there for them with love and support. Be the best role model in their lives.

Let your good character speak for itself.

We had human parents to discipline us, and we respected them. Should we not be even more willing to be subject to the Father? (Hebrews 12:9)

Father, guide me to serve as a model for my children.

Today's Tourist Attraction, Tomorrow's Cow Food

It started out as a secret because Allen Cockerline, a veteran Connecticut dairy farmer, was too embarrassed to talk about his latest cash crop—a giant maze carved into his cornfield.

But after one fall season when 2,500 visitors paid $5 each to make their way through the maze on Cockerline's 30-acre farm, he stopped caring if the other farmers were laughing at him.

Once a novelty, corn mazes can now be found on hundreds of farms across the United States. They are tourist attractions in the same way as pick-your-own apple or strawberry fields—a challenge for some; sheer fun for others.

And when the weather puts an end to the maze madness, all is not lost. After the field—and the maze it makes—is torn up, the corn is used to feed the cows.

The secret mazes of our lives, if trod diligently, can yield a good harvest. What we need is grace-filled courage.

Seek the Lord while He may be found, call upon Him while He is near. (Isaiah 55:6)

I search for You, Lord, in the moments of this day. Help me find You.

Take Me to Your Leader

What do you believe makes a good leader? While much has been written about leadership, most experts agree on four common traits of a good leader. Leaders are...

- Listeners: hearing others' suggestions and concerns.
- Encouragers: encouraging others to help bring out their best.

They are also...

- Assertive: saying what needs to be said without unkindness. They tell the truth openly and frankly.
- Decisive: making timely, even difficult decisions, as necessary but without running others' lives.

Jesus had these traits in abundance. How can you emulate Him by being a leader in at least some areas of your own life?

The government of the earth is in the hand of the Lord, and over it He will raise up the right leader for the time. (Sirach 10:4)

Lord Jesus, how may we serve others well, whether at home, work or in any other place?

Bearers of Beautiful Music

Deep in the Appalachian woods each year one can hear the sound of rhythmic toe tapping, fiddling, harmonica and banjo playing meandering through the trees. These are sounds of a another era.

At the Augusta Heritage Center in Elkins, West Virginia, musicians who intend to preserve the authentic style and technique of Appalachian folk music come to study and play with aging masters.

As one student said, "My main concern is to carry this music into the future." It's an underlying passion both teacher and apprentice share at the center.

What that is good, useful or delightful can I help preserve and carry into the future?

You were...strangers to the covenants of promise...But now in Christ Jesus you...have been brought near by the blood of Christ. (Ephesians 2:12, 13)

Lord God, help us remember what matters to us.

The Sound of a Voice

Imagine a world in which your voice can be copied and made to say things you didn't and wouldn't say.

Recently a company announced that it would start selling software that was so good at mimicking the human voice that it could be used to bring the voices of celebrities, long dead, back to life. There has been similar software before, but not of the quality that you couldn't tell it was a machine talking.

The software raises the possibility that movie studios may soon be able to give their computer-generated characters computer-generated voices. More problematic is the possibility that people may use the software to trick others into thinking they're receiving phone calls from someone that they know.

But no matter how technology advances, human beings are what will always give the human voice meaning–and, of course, ultimately something of value to say.

My sheep hear My voice. I know them, and they follow Me. (John 10:27)

Good Shepherd, how may we use our voices to praise You and to encourage one another?

Finding God in the Next Pew

Two men, barely acquainted with each other, prayed for help in the same church one October day.

Don Elliot asked God for help in finding a kidney donor for his daughter. Charles Mercurio asked the Lord to use him in some way that would give purpose to his life. The two men played in the church's volunteer musical group, yet neither knew of the other's needs before that day. Mercurio offered one of his own healthy kidneys to Elliot's ailing daughter.

There were doubts. Previous offers had evaporated when the donor learned how serious the surgery was. Mercurio took his fears to his wife and to the Lord.

With God's strength, the two men and their families walked into New York Presbyterian Hospital some months later and, literally, answered each other's prayers.

Whose prayers can you help God answer today?

Sacrifice and offering...Burnt offering and sin offering You have not required. Then I said, "...I delight to do Your will, O my God." (Psalm 40:6-7,8)

Thank You, Father, for making me a recipient of Your blessings, and an instrument of them, too.

Home Mission

The late Samuel Mockbee had long been troubled by the poverty he found in the South. So in 1993, this Mississippi architect decided to channel his concern into action by founding the Rural Studio.

Mockbee saw the Studio as a way to train a new generation of student architects in his belief that "architecture is a social art. It has to function in an ethical, moral way to help people."

Rural Studio builds affordable housing using innovative designs and local, inexpensive materials.

The house built for the Bryant family has walls made from bales of hay and acrylic. The smokehouse – they're fishermen – is made of scrapped wood and concrete from an old silo; colored bottles set in the walls draw in light. The nearby Harris house has a winged roof that earned it the nickname, "The Butterfly House."

Said Mockbee, "We are onto something good."

Appreciate your home. Make it a place of hospitality.

God gives the desolate a home to live in. (Psalm 68:6)

Shelter me in Your love, Creator. Help me to find rest in You.

"Enough Already"

Before his third cancer operation, "Good Morning America" film critic Joel Siegel thought of the Hebrew word, *dayenu:* "It means 'enough already.' That's what I was feeling– *dayenu.*"

Back at work and in reasonably good health, Siegel says the most difficult aspect of cancer is explaining it to his only child, 3-year-old Dylan. He's trying to demystify the disease by telling his son about it. "If you lie to your kids, whenever it is that they find out, it really hurts," says Siegel. He adds, "I might not be around when Dylan gets older, so I've written a history for him...I want him to know he's related to people who survived."

Dealing with dying Siegel says, has meant learning "what is important," and "you learn to prioritize, and...not to waste your time. You tell people you love them."

Now, today, who needs to hear you say, "I love you?"

The days of our life are seventy years or perhaps eighty...their span is only toil and trouble...So teach us to count our days that we may gain a wise heart. (Psalm 90:10,12)

Giver of life, we vow not to fritter away Your gift of life.

Fighting Back against Prejudice

Bonnie Jouhari, a fair-housing specialist for HUD, first experienced prejudice in 1982. Her own father shouted that she and her baby daughter would "never set foot in (his) house" and that he would have nothing to do with them because the father of her daughter was black. She knew she would have to fight racism.

Sixteen years later she and her daughter, Danielle, were forced to flee the death threats and harassment of both a neo-Nazi group and a white supremacist minister.

Finally, HUD charged the head of the neo-Nazi group with violating the Fair Housing Act. He was ordered to pay Jouhari more than $1,000,000. To avoid a trial the minister signed a conciliation agreement and apologized on his cable TV show. Still, Jouhari and her daughter had to move to a secret location and change their names.

Watch your own attitudes and actions. Prejudice has no place in a democratic nation; in an interconnected world.

You shall love your neighbor as yourself. (Matthew 19:19)

Jesus, help me respect and accept everyone.

Filing It Away

In the 1970's, Kenneth Cobb didn't imagine that he'd find his life's work among 3,000,000 pounds of historical documents.

Cobb was a student then and heard of New York City's Municipal Archives for the first time in a history class. Tax bills, birth certificates, movie film, more than 1,000,000 photographs and other material dating back as far as 1625 make up the Archives. They were neglected and largely unrecorded.

Moving from student to intern to employee, and now director of the Archives, Cobb dedicated his life to preserving and cataloging them. His efforts have rewritten portions of the city's history and been the subject of books and a television series. Enduring budget cuts and understaffing, Cobb put the rich history in his head down on paper and disk.

Every job has the opportunity to do some good for the present and the future. Seize it and make it your own.

Remember the wonderful works He has done, His miracles, and the judgments He uttered. (1 Chronicles 16:12)

Thank You, Lord, for giving me Your work to do each day.

Not Just for Vampires

Garlic ice cream. Garlic fudge. Carrot cake – with garlic frosting.

These odd-sounding treats are a feast for the Reppert family. In fact, Pat Reppert offers 98 pages of garlic recipes in her cookbook, *Mad for Garlic*. She helped found the Hudson Valley Garlic Festival in 1989. Now it draws thousands of visitors.

Pat and husband Edmund, a cardiologist, "live and breathe garlic." Each year, Edmund plants more than half a dozen varieties of garlic in eight 30-foot rows in the family's garden.

A sunny location is essential and good drainage is a plus. While garlic growers may disagree about harvest times and growing methods, all agree that planting cloves, or seed garlic, must get into the ground in October to have a crop next autumn.

Take the trouble to plan and plant for the future.

We remember...the cucumbers, the melons, the leeks, the onions and the garlic; but now...there is nothing...but this manna. (Numbers 11:5-6)

This day, Master, I will plant the seeds of joy and hope to grow gardens filled with Your love.

Holiness in the Modern World

What image does the word "saint" call to mind? If you think of early martyrs or founders of religious orders, you're right—but only up to a point.

Take Carlos Manuel Rodriguez, a twentieth century Puerto Rican layman known as Charlie. Beatified by Pope John Paul II in 2001, he created an apostolate among university students which encouraged a philosophy balancing the natural and supernatural, the ancient and the modern. More than that, Rodriguez, who had to abandon his own studies because of health problems, went to work and gave everything he earned to the poor. He died in 1963.

His reflective, generous life is worth imitating. Indeed, Pope John Paul II has said that all are called to pursue sanctity, "in a conscious and responsive way." Holiness does not just belong to other times or other people. It can be our way, if we choose it.

The fruit of the Spirit is love, joy, peace, patience, kindness, generosity, faithfulness, gentleness and self-control. (Galatians 5:22)

Jesus, beloved Friend, guide me in the path of holiness. Guide me through time and into eternity with You.

Words of Kindness Remembered

One day a teacher asked her class to write down the names of all the students in the room and list the nicest thing they could say about each one. The teacher collected their papers and compiled for each student a list of all the kind words his or her classmates had noted.

Years later, one of those students, Mark, was killed in Vietnam. The teacher and many of his former classmates attended his funeral and the luncheon that followed. During the lunch Mark's father showed the teacher a well-worn, taped together piece of paper. "They found this on Mark when he was killed," he said. "We thought you might recognize it."

It was the list of all the good things the students had written about Mark all those years before.

It's a lesson in treasuring—and telling—others the good we find in them, every day.

Remember the commandments, and do not be angry with your neighbor; remember the covenant of the Most High, and overlook faults. (Sirach 28:7)

Master, all that comes from You is good. Thank You for the blessings You give me this day through Your people.

Sailing Away

In 1995, retirees Beatrice and Robert Muller cruised around the world on the Queen Elizabeth 2. From then on, they scheduled annual trips on the boat.

In 1999 they boarded the ship for what would be their last voyage together. After 57 years of marriage, Beatrice became a widow at sea. "It was where he wanted to be," she observed.

Rather than return home, Beatrice threw caution to the wind and took up permanent residence on the QE2. She says the cost is comparable to life in a retirement home, and enjoys the city-like feeling of the vessel's shops, restaurants and entertainment.

An octogenarian, Beatrice intends to stay on the boat as long as possible. "Sometimes I feel like I've died and gone to heaven," she says. "I have to look to make sure the crew members don't have wings on their backs."

Every life has its changes and its chances. Choose well.

Even to old age and gray hairs, O God, do not forsake me, until I proclaim Your might to all the generations to come. (Psalm 71:18)

Keep us young at heart, Father, always willing to embrace new adventures.

Caring about Politics

The Lincoln-Douglas debates of 1858 are legendary for what was said – and the influence on history.

In the Illinois Senate race that year incumbent Stephen A. Douglas, a Democrat, faced Republican Abraham Lincoln for "seven impassioned political debates." One subject was slavery. Shirley Streshinsky writing in *Preservation* calls them "the most important in American history."

Each three hour debate went on despite the weather. "Major newspapers sent reporters adept at shorthand to record the debates verbatim and transmit them via…telegraph, so the entire nation could follow along."

Thousands of spectators arrived on foot, horse, by canal boats, special trains and wagons for the debates.

That 19th century level of citizens' involvement in politics gives us food for thought. We, too, need to be interested and active in government matters.

Unless the Lord guards the city, the guard keeps watch in vain. (Psalm 127:1)

Inspire citizens to peaceful and intelligent involvement in the political process, Lord of the Nations.

Finding a Pal

Ataxia-telangiectasia, known as A-T, is a very rare genetic disease that causes neurological deterioration and death.

Joe Kindegran, 14, is one of those battling A-T, and now a well-known friend is helping him in his fight to survive.

A few years ago, Kindegran's mom took him and his sister, Stacy, to Dulles Airport to watch actor Ben Affleck film scenes for a movie. Affleck saw Kindegran in his electric wheelchair, came over to say hello and the two became friends.

This led Affleck to become involved in fund-raising in the search for a cure for A-T. Says Affleck who has lobbied Congress for research money, "it seems particularly unfair when something happens to a kid who hasn't had the chance to experience life." He adds, "I'm waiting for a happy ending."

Life has no guarantees, but the more we contribute to the well-being of others, the greater our opportunity for happiness

The God of all grace...will Himself restore, support, strengthen, and establish you. (1 Peter 5:10)

Help me bear the trials of life with dignity, Lord Christ.

Manual Versus Machine

Robert A. Caro, a Pulitzer Prize winning author, still uses a typewriter. "I'm not saying computers are a bad thing," he says, "but for me, the very act of going slower gives you more time to think about it. And I am always afraid that I won't think enough."

Pro-typewriter proponents cite specific advantages: a typewriter will not "crash," causing the loss of work; there are no software upgrades. Also, computer users are more prone to carpal tunnel syndrome.

On the other hand, writers like Andy Rooney of TV's "60 Minutes" say computers have improved their work. "I now redo things that I wouldn't have taken the time to redo," he says. Yet he still owns several typewriters for envelopes and thank you notes.

While the debate continues, one fact is true: the written word matters and needs to be treated with intelligence.

The word of God is living and active, sharper than any two-edged sword...able to judge the thoughts and intentions of the heart. (Hebrews 4:12)

Your word is truth and life, Lord. Help me to know the words to say, words that will change hearts and lives.

Channeling Grief to Help All

Journalist Autumn Alexander Skeen always believed in auto safety for children. So when she buckled her 4-year-old son Anton in the front of her SUV next to her, she felt she was doing the right thing.

But on that 1996 day Skeen had an accident. As she lay in the hospital with serious injuries, she learned that her little boy had been thrown from the SUV and killed.

Skeen channeled her grief into being an advocate for child car safety. She lobbied and campaigned for car "booster seats" to bridge the gap between child car seats and the adult seat belt system. Today, her home state, Washington, has the first booster-seat initiative, and advocates say federal legislation is pending.

Skeen's crusade in memory of Anton has renewed her. As she sees it, "What would make me feel most guilty is if I sat at home grieving without trying to save other parents from this."

Use both your sorrows and your joys for the good of others.

Grief may result in death, and a sorrowful heart saps one's strength. (Sirach 38:18)

Help me to protect children, Child Jesus.

Lady of Possibilities

Popular daytime talk show host Oprah Winfrey appeared in four different cities in four daylong seminars called the "Live Your Best Life Tour." Oprah imparted her inspirational mix of wisdom directly to fans, mostly women, whom she told, "I'm just like you. I'm a woman in progress."

Winfrey told the audience that we are co-creators of our lives, but that there is definitely a "higher power," a force greater than each of us. Believing in something bigger than yourself is key to becoming the person you want to be. "Constantly listen and try to be obedient to the calling," she counseled.

Winfrey is one public personality who believes in the power of prayer. Her fans are inspired by her and think of her as a messenger, and the message is one of positive uplift. As one fan said, Winfrey has shown her "all things are possible."

God gives us more than we ever know, especially love.

For God all things are possible. (Mark 10:27)

Spirit, guide me to live my passion and give to others.

The Good in Gander

On September 11, 2001, as terrorist attacks killed thousands in New York City, Washington, D.C. and Pennsylvania, the skies were shut down. An Atlanta bound Delta flight and 52 others were told to land in Newfoundland.

Passengers and crew were eventually bused into Gander. The town of 10,400 welcomed 10,500 passengers. High schools, meeting halls and other gathering places became mass hotels. Elderly passengers were taken to private homes and locals prepared food for guests or took them to eateries.

That Saturday as they resumed their flight to Atlanta, passengers swapped stories of the good they had discovered in Gander. A doctor asked for pledges to a trust fund he would set up. Passengers pledged more than $14,500 for scholarships for Gander's high school students.

Brought together by evil, people found a lot of good. And good is always stronger than evil.

The alien...shall be to you as the citizen...love the alien as yourself, for you were aliens in...Egypt. (Leviticus 19:34)

Help me, Lord, to bring Your goodness to a waiting world.

Unconditional Love

Dogs give us unconditional love, so it makes sense that "canine candy-stripers" are being used in increasing numbers in hospitals everywhere. They provide "creature" comfort when we humans need it most.

What began two decades ago as recreation for patients has today become an important component of patient care. And it's not just dogs helping: cerebral palsy patients like to ride horses, nursing home residents find therapy in cats, and burn victims are comforted by the soft fur of chinchillas.

Animals can lift the spirits of heart-transplant patients during the months they spend waiting for an organ. One patient, attached to an IV and other high-tech machinery, was able to keep his big German shepherd by his side. As the dog nuzzled her master lovingly, he said, "She is life. Like sun and air."

God is the source of love. He has generously provided human beings and fellow companion animals to feel His touch.

Let love be genuine...love one another with mutual affection. (Romans 12:9,10)

Bless our loving beasts and watch over them, Creator.

Physician, Soldier, Hero, Woman

In a *U.S. News & World Report* article, Americans said they expected "heroes to persevere despite adversity, to go beyond expectations, to stay level-headed in a crisis, and to risk themselves for...a better society."

That's a good description of Colonel Rhonda Cornum, a U.S. Army flight surgeon.

On Feb. 27, 1991, then Major Cornum tried to rescue Air Force Capt. Bill Andrews behind Iraqi lines. Her helicopter was shot down. She spent eight days as a Gulf War POW. Both her arms had been broken; a knee shattered. There was a bullet in her right shoulder. An Iraqi guard assaulted her, but she did not reveal classified information during repeated interrogations.

Not only do heroes like Col. Cornum go beyond the call of duty and put themselves at risk, they also remind all of us about our calling to our higher selves.

Who are your heroes in the wars against crime, disease, poverty, prejudice and pollution?

Be courageous and valiant. (2 Samuel 13:28)

Bless our everyday heroes, Father.

Plain and Simple Labels

Here's a welcome change. From now on, you won't need to translate "albumen" to egg white and "casein" to milk when you're reading food labels at the grocery store.

Simple, straightforward language will be of great help to the nearly 7 million Americans who suffer from food allergies. Industry groups had called for labeling guidelines that consisted of "plain English," rather than the obscure terms commonly used. The new labels will also provide specific descriptions of any allergens. After all, avoidance is the only option for people with food allergies, which lead to 30,000 emergency-room visits and 150 to 200 deaths a year.

A common-sense approach when it comes to language is a refreshing and practical change.

In a complex world, simplicity and clarity benefit all.

Let your word be 'Yes, Yes' or 'No, No'; anything more than this comes from the evil one. (Matthew 5:37)

Enable me to communicate clearly and honestly, Spirit.

Moving On

At 19, Mary Geis jumped up on a trampoline during a college gym class and severed her spine, paralyzing her from the neck down.

"God and I have had lots of talks," she says, admitting that her faith has helped get her through her darkest moments during the three decades that have passed since her tragic accident.

A resident of the Mequon Care Center in Wisconsin for all these years, Mary doesn't indulge in self-pity–"that gets old fast," she says. Instead, she has aided others, especially younger patients at the Center. "I can't take away all their worries, but if I can help even a little bit, then I'm happy," she says.

"Mary has helped a lot of people through some very difficult times," says Jim Lehmkuhl, Mequon's executive director. "She gives from the heart."

You don't have to move a finger to touch someone's heart.

The Lord God...will feed his flock like a shepherd... gather the lambs in His arms, and carry them in His bosom. (Isaiah 40:10,11)

In stillness and silence, You are there, Father, comforting and consoling me.

Breaking the "Can't" Barrier

In 1954, Britain's Roger Bannister electrified the world when he broke the four-minute mile barrier. He refused to believe what so many others said, that running a mile in under four minutes was humanly impossible. His breakthrough proved that the barrier was psychological, not physiological.

A contemporary runner, Dr. Jerry Lynch, insists that when you believe and think you can, you put into gear your motivation, commitment, confidence and concentration. He believes that the path to personal excellence, in sports and in life, is filled with obstacles, but that those obstacles can stretch our limits.

Failing can serve as a positive experience in that it helps improve our performance. What's more, each of us grows stronger, physically, mentally and spiritually, when we are tested with resistance or opposition.

If we hope for what we do not see, we wait for it with patience. (Romans 8:25)

Spirit of Fortitude, enable me to always believe that I can!

A Chore a Day...

Did you know that putting off chores can actually make you sick? According to Dianne Tice, a psychology professor at Case Western Reserve University, the stress from procrastinating weakens the immune system.

It's relatively easy to make a list, but how often do we follow through on plans we have made? One way to stay healthy and get those pesky chores done in time to do our favorite things is to enlist support. Don't be afraid to ask for help if your list is overwhelming. Turn a chore into time to catch up on the latest events with your spouse, children or friends. Try to do tasks in a room where you can all work together, keep each other motivated and enjoy each other's company.

Collaboration can make the most difficult tasks seem lighter. The important thing is to finish what you set out to do.

Two are better than one...if they fall, one will lift up the other...And...two will withstand one. (Ecclesiastes 4:9,10,12)

Lord, grant me the perseverance to finish that which I have started and the courage to seek help when I need it.

Making House Calls

Dr. Kathryn Rensenbrink transferred her medical practice from San Francisco to rural Maine. She relishes the results.

"I've traded the safety and authority of anonymity for membership in a community." She embraces the chance to know her patients as neighbors and friends. "At the curve in the road by the beach lies Bridgett's house," she says. "I visit occasionally to enjoy tea and fruitcake, her late husband Dan's favorite."

The night Dan died, Dr. Rensenbrink had stopped by to comfort him and his family, at the same time "feeling puny before the unknowable."

After the funeral, the doctor received a note from Dan's widow, Bridgett, and their daughter, "thanking me for my visit, 'for coming like a guardian spirit out of the winter dark.'"

It was a moving moment: "How wonderful to be most appreciated when you feel the least able," she says.

Nurture your membership in your community.

Physician(s) pray to the Lord that He grant them success in diagnosis and in healing. (Sirach 38:12,14)

Increase my trust in how You use me, Lord.

The Joy of Age and Work

Sir John Mortimer isn't getting any younger. Nearly 80, the playwright, novelist, screenwriter and raconteur, is unsteady on his feet and losing his eyesight—but that isn't stopping him.

On the contrary, the man best known for creating that pugnacious barrister, *Rumpole of the Bailey,* is, in his latest book, *The Summer of a Dormouse,* using the tribulations of age as the stuff of comedy. In it he describes life when the body is failing but the mind is young.

Nor does he let his complaints slow him down. In one year, he co-wrote a screenplay with Franco Zeffirelli, presided over an historical preservation committee, adapted a book for television and went on a book tour.

Sir John has no hobbies: work is his leisure. He says, "otherwise I'd get terribly bored. I wouldn't know what to do."

Do as much of what you love as you can.

This is what I have seen to be good...all to whom God gives wealth and possession and whom He enables to enjoy them, and...their toil. (Ecclesiastes 5:18,19)

Creator, help me enjoy using the intelligence, personality, talents and abilities with which You have blessed me.

Back to Basics

It's no secret that millions of parents are concerned about their children's ability to spell. And rightly so, says education researcher Louisa Moats, who confirms that spelling problems are very common in today's classroom.

"Educators have been convinced that teaching spelling is stifling," says Moats, the author of three books on reading. "But it's just the opposite." She believes it can be taught in an interesting way using the history of words, sounds of letters and patterns in language. She also advocates weekly spelling tests from second grade on, and says children are surprisingly responsive to good instruction when they get it.

Is there hope for those who need help with spelling? Moats advises getting a good dictionary and making friends with it.

It seems that with spelling, with many aspects of life, the basics are *the* foundation for success.

A wise man...built his house on rock. The rain fell, the floods came and the winds blew...but it did not fall. (Matthew 7:24-25)

Master Builder, show us how to lay good foundations for our lives.

Make the Connection!

Psychoneuroimmunology may look a little intimidating, but it's simply the technical word for a re-emerging field of medicine.

Hyphens may be helpful: *psycho–neuro–immunology*. It's the study of the interconnectedness of the mind, the brain, and the immune system, according to Dr. Ralph Golan.

Scientists are now documenting how stress, emotions, and personalities affect the immune system. In other words, writes Golan, "what we think and feel, how we perceive and react, and what we believe in all have a profound effect on the health of our bodies."

Medicine men and shamans have used this knowledge to benefit their patients for centuries.

In the modern age, when exercise and good nutrition are so central to good health, it's helpful to recognize that a positive approach to life is also advantageous.

Cast your burden on the Lord, and He will sustain you. (Psalm 55:22)

Bless medical professionals, Creator, with insight and inspiration.

Dads and Daughters

Joe Kelly, the father of twin daughters and a lecturer on fatherhood, challenges fathers of daughters to answer a few questions. Do they know their daughters' school projects? Can they name their daughters' best friends? Do they spend at least a half-hour of uninterrupted time with their daughters every day?

Kelly makes these suggestions for dads:

- Focus on what's important to your daughter, what she thinks and believes, what she dreams and does, not how she looks.

- Encourage your daughter's strengths in order to help her overcome barriers and achieve goals.

- Participate with her in sports: catch or tag, jumping rope, shooting hoops, walking, hiking, skating, etc.

- Be involved. Volunteer in her activities: Coach her team; direct her play; teach a class.

Fathers, your daughters—and your sons—need your example, love and involvement every single day.

No women (were) so beautiful as Job's daughters; and their father gave them an inheritance along with their brothers. (Job 42:15)

Father, inspire family members to cherish each other.

Drawing Near

Anthony Jones has loved drawing since childhood. As a young adult, he was a commercial artist, whose clients ranged from restaurants to private commissions.

Now he is bringing life to prison walls including those of Rikers Island. Jones has created murals on command-post walls and scenes of gardens and lakes to improve visitors' areas.

"I like light so much," he told the *New York Times*. "I guess it's the space. The birds flying. Freedom." Jones understands the longing for freedom. Addicted to cocaine, he is not only an artist but also an inmate. But he is trying to beat his addiction in a drug-treatment program. Should he succeed, his marketable artistic abilities will help him rebuild his life outside.

God has given each of us talents. What are yours? What prevents you from using them for your own good and others'?

I have filled him...with ability, intelligence, and knowledge...to devise artistic designs, to work in gold, silver, and bronze, in cutting stones...in carving wood, in every kind of craft.
(Exodus 31:3,4-5)

Savior, help us to break the chains which bind our use of Your gifts and talents.

The Real Heroic Man

It's been said that a hero is a man who does what he can.

That brand of simple heroism was practiced over and over again during World War II, and Tom Brokaw, the renowned TV anchorman, has reminded us all of the sacrifices made by so many people during and after the war through the trio of books he's written about *The Greatest Generation*. Sadly, every day now about 1200 veterans of that war pass away.

Brokaw thinks of heroes as "ordinary people doing extraordinary things for the greater good."

That kind of heroism is a noble goal we can all strive to achieve in order to make it a better–and more peaceful–world. Our children and their children are counting on us.

Take courage, all you people...says the Lord; work, for I am with you, says the Lord of hosts. (Haggai 2:4)

Spirit of Courage, guide me to be the best man or woman I can be and to encourage others to be the best they can, too.

A Trees Grows in Dallas

Every fall since 1987, Jesuit priest John Stack and many volunteers have been planting trees in Dallas.

The first year, the group planted about 88 trees on a high school campus. Since then, hundreds of people have gathered every year on a November Sunday to plant hundreds of trees.

Rev. Stack says word about the activity has gotten out and, because the volunteers come from many places–churches, synagogues, high schools, scout troops, and more–the event is now very ecumenical.

The project began as a way to celebrate Thanksgiving. And the people of Dallas certainly appreciate the beauty the thousands of trees added to their city.

Look around and consider the many things people do to improve the world–for which we should express our thanks.

O Lord, how manifold are your works! (Psalm 104:24)

Gather us in, Lord, bind us together in love of You and love for one another.

From Gloom to Cheer

One August while on vacation, Virginia and John Kippes met a couple with whom they had an immediate rapport. They exchanged addresses and telephone numbers to stay in touch and to plan a vacation together.

A few days before Thanksgiving, Virginia was home from work recuperating from a cold and feeling tired and sad. She had invited the family for the holiday and did not want to cancel the invitation. Then she received a floral arrangement for her Thanksgiving table, something she had never had. Its bright colors reawakened her usual optimism and cheerfulness.

The thoughtful couple that they had met in August sent the flowers because Virginia had told them she always asked John's family to their house to celebrate Thanksgiving.

When we say let's keep in touch, do we? It could mean so much to others, as well as to ourselves.

Better is a neighbor who is nearby than kindred who are far away. (Proverbs 27:10)

Holy Paraclete, inspire me to be a person of my word, and a person of generosity, as well.

Open Wide the Door

Grace Crews made the extraordinary leap from getting to know Tommy, a lonely stranger, to inviting him to live with her family when he lost his apartment. She knew his only other option was homelessness.

Crews and her family took care of the octogenarian on and off for the next eight years, until he died. During that time, Tommy came to know many neighbors, including three-year-old Canaan Crawford, who developed a special closeness with the old man.

"I won't say it was easy," Grace says of her family's commitment, "but I don't remember it being hard."

Eleven years after Tommy died, Canaan, then a bright, good-natured young man, lost his life in an automobile accident. Grace Crews finds comfort in the thought of Tommy watching over him. "I bet the two of them still have a lot to talk about."

We don't always know how much our lives and our love mean to others. But they do.

**God did not make death, and He does not delight in the death of the living.
(Wisdom of Solomon 1:13)**

How deftly You weave our lives together, Lord.

A Simple Thank You

When a child receives something, whether an object or a compliment, he or she is told, "Say 'thank you'." And that's exactly what the youngster says.

As adults, sometimes we forget the concise graciousness of "thank you" and insist on adding to it.

Unfortunately, some people add disparaging phrases. No one likes being told, "You shouldn't have," "I've had it for years," or "I really didn't do anything special." The intent is to be modest but the fact is, it's insensitive.

Let's use words we would like to hear to express our gratitude, or let's just say thank you.

And while we're on the subject, "you're welcome" is a welcome phrase, too.

Sing to the Lord with thanksgiving.
(Psalm 147:7)

Abba, all good things come through You. I pray that all Your children accept them with graciousness.

A Corner on Miracles

Just before Thanksgiving in 1988, Jeannie Jaybush was appalled to learn of the high infant-mortality and poverty rate right in her own Seattle neighborhood.

She decided to do something. She placed an empty box in a corner of St. Joseph's Church and asked the pastor to announce a collection drive for baby supplies. The box was full in three hours. In the first year, the "Baby Corner" helped 80 families.

More than a decade later, more than 60 organizations depend on the Baby Corner, which last year gave away some $320,000 worth of baby items to about 2,700 families. Jeannie Jaybush continues to be the leader in the effort, logging 40 to 60 unpaid hours each week.

"I can't change the world, stop world hunger or crime, but I can do a few little things," she says. "A lot of little things add up."

Do a little something today for someone else. And be sure to show your gratitude to those who have done little things for you.

Walk in the way of the good, and keep to the paths of the just. (Proverbs 2:20)

With every breath, I thank You, Lord, for You have given me so many gifts.

Helping Save Others

Richard and Leticia Berrelez want to be remembered as grandparents "who cared for the safety and protection of children."

The Colorado couple's granddaughter, Alie, had been abducted and killed. Leticia Berrelez said they had to do something positive with their shattered emotions to prevent it from happening again.

Within days the Berrelez's began A.L.I.E. (Abducted, Lost, Innocent and Enough) Foundation, which donates trained search dogs to jurisdictions that can't afford them. The highly successful organization has donated more than 100 dogs to law enforcement agencies in 26 states.

Leticia Berrelez, speaking for all those who have unspeakable pain, said, "We all hurt. But we have to go on." Training and lending search dogs is one way to do that.

We do have to go on. How we do so is up to us.

Overcome evil with good. (Romans 12:21)

I will make the most of this moment in time, Forgiving Lord.

Another Kind of Hero

Usually when we envision heroes we see sports or historical or mythological figures. But for novelist James Salter, the hero is personified by his old friend and fellow novelist, Ben Sonnenberg, Jr.

Years ago, shortly after they met, Sonnenberg began displaying early signs of multiple sclerosis. Year by year, all of Sonnenberg's physical capabilities were destroyed. Everything had to be done for him, yet he never complained. He never spoke of the injustice of what had befallen him, and he never despaired or let others pity him. Instead, he founded and edited a literary magazine, saw many people at his home, and celebrated each birthday with a party.

Salter admits to being jealous of Sonnenberg's bravery and spirit. As Salter puts it poetically, a hero "is one crushed...(but) despite it, triumphs."

Heroes are not necessarily defined by success, but by the struggle.

Be courageous and valiant. (2 Samuel 13:28)

Thank You for the spirit and will to go on, Lion of Judah.

Putting the Rest Back in Sundays

What do you do on Sunday? Clean out the garage. Catch up on bills and paper work. Run errands or run to the nearest shopping mall?

That used to be the way the Kenisons spent the Sabbath, but not anymore. "What we all need is to stop moving," says Katrina Kenison.

For the past year, Katrina, her husband and their two sons have made Sundays special, setting their "to do" lists aside. The family goes to church "after years of believing that we didn't have time for church," says Katrina. After that, the day is up for grabs. "We may take a walk in the woods or putter around the yard," she says. "We may even read the 10-pound newspaper we pick up on the way home from church."

The Sabbath should be a day not just "to do," but "to be" in the Lord.

It is lawful to do good on the Sabbath. (Matthew 12:12)

You have given us this day, Creator. May our actions praise You.

'Tis a Gift to Be Simple

Maryland's Center for a New American Dream found that 92 percent of Americans believe people spend more money on the holiday season than they can afford. Another 82 percent would prefer receiving a family photo album to a store-bought gift. Yet average consumers spend nearly $1000 on holiday gifts.

Bill McKibben, author of *Hundred Dollar Holiday*, offers an alternative. His family has found joy exchanging gifts including handmade walking sticks and handpainted plates. In his book he avoids the tightwad mindset, instead focusing on values.

He suggests asking the simple question: "Is this making you as happy as you think it is?"

What a great subject for families or friends to discuss prior to the rush of the holidays.

Removed from the hustle and bustle, perhaps you, too, would like to find ways to celebrate the holidays in a less expensive yet more meaningful fashion.

Life does not consist in the abundance of possessions. (Luke 12:15)

Inspire us, Lord, to share ourselves more fully.

Stopping Breast Cancer Today

Nothing in her experience had prepared "Today Show" anchor Ann Curry for the shock she felt on learning that her younger sister, Jean, had breast cancer.

"It was devastating," recalls Curry. While another sister, Lola, helped Jean get to medical appointments, Ann did what she does best: she worked the phones and grilled renowned breast cancer specialists to ensure her sister was getting the right treatments. Curry also increased her efforts on behalf of breast cancer organizations. She continues to report on the subject for "Today." She says, "I want so much to help and do better and do more for these women."

Following a difficult regimen of treatment, Curry's sister has recovered and is cancer free. As one observer put it, "Ann's impact on breast cancer awareness has been invaluable. A sister's love is not only deep and enduring, but...a force that saves lives."

Show your love in useful ways.

Jesus loved Martha and her sister. (John 11:5)

May I always help those in need, especially family, Father.

Homeless Customers

Restaurateur Phil Romano has netted millions from his theme eateries such as *Fuddruckers* and *Romano's Macaroni Grill*. But his latest success is dear to his heart.

Realizing that "there was still one customer I hadn't served–probably the most important one," Romano hatched his latest venture: a restaurant on wheels called *Hunger Busters* that serves freshly prepared soups and sandwiches to hundreds of homeless in Dallas, Texas. The operation's lead ladler is Romano, ably assisted in the truck by wife Lillie, son Sam, 5, and other helpers. "It's my way of giving back," says the multimillionaire.

Romano could have written checks to homeless shelters and been done with it, but he made a choice to be in the thick of things, helping out and feeding those in dire need.

We can all make a choice to reach out and help. Do so today, and feed your heart and soul.

Do not neglect to do good and to share what you have. (Hebrews 13:16)

Lord, guide me to help the needy.

Be Smart When Giving

It is better to give than to receive, but better still to give wisely. With all the charities available, it is not always easy to choose. One thing is certain: Americans are generous, on average giving about 3 percent of their income to charity.

Yet, financial expert Andrew Tobias asks, "if you are financially blessed, how about giving 10 percent or 20 percent? ...Think about what (your money) could do for a worthy cause."

He likens picking charities to picking a portfolio of stocks in that you want a great return on your social investment. You want the bulk of your contribution to go to the people or cause it's intended to help. You might want to assess larger charities by taking a look at web sites that specialize in this information.

As the year winds down, consider how you can make your money work to help make a difference for a worthy cause.

When you give alms, do not let your left hand know what your right hand is doing. (Matthew 6:3)

Inspire me to be willing, Compassionate Lord, to make my material goods count for others.

Good Eggs

One person can make a difference. That is the basis for the *Catholic Digest's* "Good Egg Awards." Readers are asked to nominate everyday people who give of themselves in uncommon ways–in other words, the "good eggs" in our communities.

Take Nancy Watt, one year's first place winner. A friend, Silvija Perija, who had fled the war in Sarajevo and finally settled in Ontario, Canada, nominated her.

Perija's little boy, Dario, was introduced to the English language by Watt who, according to Perija, enriched her son's and all the students' lives with attention and care. Watt supports all her students' talents and gifts, even attending events such as concerts or soccer games to offer encouragement.

Each of us can make a difference. Be a good egg today.

How can I help you? (Baruch 4:17)

Imbue me with the spirit of helping others, young and old, friend and stranger, Lord Jesus.

Family Healing and Reconnecting

The Holiday season is fast approaching. Sadly, not everyone is planning to celebrate with family. Personal slights, long-harbored resentments and ongoing feuding have severed ties and caused ongoing disharmony for all too many.

Dr. Joyce Brothers suggests that family feuds can be healed with the help of a mediator. If you are acting as a go-between, here are some steps she recommends:

- Don't wait. Enough time has gone by.
- Don't play favorites. Ask each to see the other's viewpoint.
- Share happy memories.
- Look to the future. Point out that life and time is too short for all of us.

First and foremost, nothing brings families together faster than forgiveness. Forgive, and watch the anger dissipate and reconnecting begin.

Please forgive the trespass of your servant. (1 Samuel 25:28)

May I forgive trespasses as You forgive me, Father.

A Soldier's Best Friend, too

In 1943, when General George Patton's army came ashore on the beaches of Sicily under deafening naval bombardment, they had a GI who could hear and smell things no ordinary soldier could detect. His name: Chips. He was one of thousands of dogs in the Army's K-9 Corps, which had been established at the start of World War II.

Chips helped defend his soldier-handler. When the soldier was pinned down under heavy machine-gun fire, Chips broke free and raced to the source of the fire. An enemy soldier, with Chips tearing at his throat and arms, emerged. So did several others.

The dog had powder burns on his coat. His scalp had been wounded. But 'his' soldier had survived. Chips had joined the dogs who have served and saved lives in wars since bow-and-arrow times – and continue to do so today.

Above all, remember all the men and women who have given their strength and courage, their very lives for the protection of their families and countries.

The Lord of hosts will protect them. (Zechariah 9:15)

All life is precious, Lord. Remind us to value it each moment.

Through the Open Door

This Christmas season open some doors. This is the advice of Sister Joyce Rupp, O.S.M., who reflects, "Doors provide a passageway to where we want to go...Doors are also instruments of power. They have the ability to shut out or admit in."

She says that Advent is a season for opening doors. It is a "time to deepen and strengthen our relationship with the Holy One so that more of the divine presence within us shines through and offers a welcome to others."

Fear can keep us from opening the doors that need to be opened, and there's often a price for such openness: confusion, doubt and unsettledness, as well as the possibility of being hurt by others. Opening a door may involve going "the extra mile," but in the end we receive much more than we have given. Sometimes fear is a necessary protection against real danger and discernment is needed, but often we hide behind doors that should be opened.

Do not fear, for I am with you. (Isaiah 43:5)

Show me the door You want me to open, Newborn Jesus. Share Your courage with me that I may walk through that opened door into a fuller life.

The Toughest Opponent

Rising tennis star Corina Morariu was used to battling tough opponents across the net, but her current foe has truly tested the young woman. It's also provided her a new perspective on life.

After being ranked the number one doubles player in women's tennis, Morariu began feeling "blah." Before long, nosebleeds began to occur and soon after she was told the dreadful news: she was very sick with acute leukemia.

After months of aggressive treatment and with constant support from family and friends, Morariu is doing well. For now, she's concentrating on her health and on her future. Calling what's happened to her "a wake-up call," she says with wisdom beyond her years, "I realize the important things now are your health and family and friends. Just having the people you love and who love you, that can't be beat."

Prize what is truly important in your life.

Where your treasure is, there your heart will be also. (Matthew 6:21)

Help me keep my spirits high in the face of woes, Lord.

Not Now! It's My 10-Minute Vacation!

Every few hours, writer Lisa Belkin pauses for a vacation of sorts. Her travel destination? Her computer's Minesweeper game. After a few minutes she returns to the real world, refreshed and ready to work.

Doug Renfro, president of a family-owned salsa manufacturing business in Fort Worth, Texas, offers: "I sometimes go to expedia.com or travelocity.com and plan a fantasy trip, like to Switzerland. It takes maybe five minutes, is interesting and it relieves stress."

Angela Henry, a partner in an executive search firm in New York, visits old lobbies to marvel at the architecture. Tom Dilatush, chief executive of a San Diego technology company, saves particularly pleasant tasks, like telling someone about a promotion or a bonus, for his breaks.

While not a replacement for the honest-to-goodness-out-of-the-office experience, these small time-outs are just as necessary to refresh body and mind and relieve the stress of the day.

Therefore do not worry. (Matthew 6:31)

In the silence, I find You, Lord, bringing me comfort, giving me strength.

Portraits of a People

Historian, photographer and MacArthur "genius" award winner Deborah Willis is committed to documenting the black experience in America, including her own.

Willis' father, a policeman, was a serious amateur photographer whose work included pictures of neighbors, such as the women who visited her mother's hair salon. Her earliest memories are of watching in the darkroom as the pictures developed seemingly by magic.

Ms. Willis' professional work includes having curated an important show, "Reflections in Black: a History of Black Photographers, 1840 to the Present." Sadly, on the eve of its opening, her nephew, who was on his way there, was held up and shot to death.

"This was a nonviolent kid," said Ms. Willis. "I want to use some of the MacArthur money to do a project about gun violence."

As with any tragedy, one can try to make good come of it.

For everything there is a season, and time for every matter under heaven. (Ecclesiastes 3:1)

May senseless deaths and random violence spur us to work for peace with justice, Just Judge.

To Thine Own Cloth Be True

It's not that Donald John MacKay has anything against hot pink. It's just that he intends to remain true to himself

MacKay is one of the traditional weavers on Scotland's Isle of Harris. Having apprenticed with his father at eight, the craftsman nowworks at his cast iron loom six days a week He produces at least 25 yards a day of the scratchy, knotty, much-prized cloth known the world over as Harris Tweed. Earthen shades of gray, brown, plum, and dark green come out of his clattering loom.

The winds of change have begun to sway some weavers on the Isle of Harris. Colors including pink and turquoise are showing up in new patterns. "The women's wear market is huge, and we're going for it," says mill owner Derick Murray.

MacKay is not disturbed, but he remains focused. "I know what my customers want," he says.

How precious is your steadfast love, O God! (Psalm 36:7)

Lord, give us the wisdom to know ourselves and to persevere, even when others are called elsewhere.

New Family Ties

Holiday time is family time and often, family conflict time.

One common source of conflict occurs when so-called "adult children" seek to change the terms of their relationship with parents. In some homes, Christmas is a particularly sensitive time as members of the younger generation try to establish their own holiday rituals while not neglecting their families of origin and the older generation.

In the year that psychotherapist Kelsey Menehan turned 40, she changed her routine and spent Christmas with close friends. But she still worried that she was being disloyal to her parents.

Menehan recognizes "the pain of...being apart and reconnecting in a different way. But there's a poignancy too, and a sense of God's presence in the many ties that bind me to family and friends."

With enough good will on the part of all involved, the changes can happen in a way that ultimately benefits all.

Ascribe to the Lord...glory and strength...the glory due His name. (Psalm 96:7,8)

Creator, bless our families.

Laugh, It's Good for You

It has long been said that laughter is the best medicine. Studies now show this to be more than just an old saying.

Stress in our lives can lead to clogged arteries by creating damage to the protective lining in blood vessels and allowing fat and cholesterol to build up.

There's nothing funny about that.

But researchers think laughter might protect against heart disease because of its link to stress reduction, according to the American Heart Association.

"We know that exercising, not smoking, and eating foods low in saturated and trans fats will reduce the risk of heart disease," said researcher Dr. Michael Miller. "Perhaps," he adds, "regular, hearty laughter should be added to the list."

Now that's something to smile about.

Our mouth was filled with laughter, and our tongue with shouts of joy. (Psalm 126:2)

Help us cope with stress, Divine Physician.

Dreaming...Succeeding

Working hard to provide better opportunities for their children has always been a part of immigrants' American Dream.

For eight years, for 13 hours a day, Yolanda and Rogelio Garcia have combed Los Angeles dumpsters for recyclables to keep their family of five going. Originally from Mexico, they are now U.S. citizens and live frugally so they can save money for their children's education.

"There's no price you can put on what they've done for me and my brother," says daughter Adrianne, a student at the University of California at Riverside. Her brother, Rogelio Jr., who will graduate from MIT, wonders how his parents do it, but hopes to contribute through an internship with a large corporation.

As the Garcias see it, "Our only dream for them is to get degrees and get ahead in life."

With hard work, persistence and powerful dreams, good things can happen.

Human success is in the hand of the Lord. (Sirach 10:5)

Guide me to love and do all for my family, Father.

Making the Season Merry

There are myriad ways to celebrate the holiday season, which have nothing to do with a buying frenzy. Try these:

- List, then enjoy, things you think would make for a joyous season–time with friends, a calm Christmas Eve, a beautiful tree.
- Share holiday memories with others.
- Send a video, which includes tree shopping, a child's holiday recital, the family singing a carol finale to a distant loved one.
- Make amends with someone. Ask forgiveness. Give it.
- Pray for each sender of your holiday cards.
- Pool the money you and your friends would spend on each other for a charitable contribution.

Give yourself the gift of joy and share it with others, especially the grieving. Be good to yourself and those around you.

Comfort all who mourn. (Isaiah 61:2)

How, Son of God, can I celebrate Your birthday?

Sacrificing for a Stranger

When Cristina Hunt and Jennifer Stoelting met for the first time, the stakes were life and death.

Both women had kidney disease and were in dire need of transplants. If their meeting went well, doctors would later remove one healthy kidney from each of the two husbands, then implant those kidneys into their ideally matched recipients.

The perfect stranger-to-stranger donation went off without a hitch. David Hunt's kidney was implanted in Jennifer Stoelting, and her husband Will's in Christina Hunt. As a doctor put it, "These husbands gave these wives at least 10 additional years."

All four are said be doing fine. They have formed what they believe will be a lifetime bond. Says Will Stoelting's stepfather, "These husbands gave their hearts to their wives when they were married. They gave their kidneys to continue that love."

Remember how inseparable love and life are.

Be kind to one another, tenderhearted. (Ephesians 4:32)

May I love all people as You love us, Christ Jesus.

Can We Talk?

"Pick up the phone and tell him, in a clear, honest way, that you wish he would spend more time with you."

That's what *My Generation* advice columnist Amy Bloom offered to parents upset because their married son spent holidays and vacations with his in-laws–and not them. "It is possible that he doesn't prefer his wife's family, but that she and they are inseparable," Bloom continues. "Or it might be that his wife's family is more demanding, and of the two sides, yours is the easier to disappoint. Or maybe your relationship with your son needs building or rebuilding in other ways."

A telephone call can open the lines of communication–and offer you both a place to start on the road back to being together, Bloom believes.

So next time you find difficulty with an adult child, parent, relative or friend, sit down and talk or pick up the phone. It's amazing what can happen when we just make an effort.

Blessed are the merciful, for they will receive mercy. (Matthew 5:7)

Lord, You are always there to comfort me. Show me how to share that comfort.

'Tis the Season to Be Stressed Out?

As much as adults complain about Christmas holiday season stress–long lines at the malls, traffic, too little time–they're not the only ones who feel it. Dr. Loraine Stern, a pediatrician, says children can also feel holiday stress.

Dr. Stern offers these tips to help both parents and youngsters enjoy the holidays:

- Avoid travel; stay close to home.
- Plan a quiet Christmas at home, phone loved ones, and schedule visits for less frantic times.
- Rein in giving. Dr. Stern believes that in some homes it's the parents who give multiple, lavish gifts.
- Remind children of how much they already have. Help them give toys to a local charity or children's hospital.

The holidays should focus on time with the people you love. Use some of that time to tell children about the spiritual dimensions of Christmas.

Wise men from the East...knelt down and paid Him homage. Then...they offered Him gifts of gold, frankincense, and myrrh. (Matthew 2:1,11)

Jesus, You came to share Your life with us. May we share our lives with our loved ones.

The Puzzle of Autism

Until he was about 18 months old, Dov smiled and happily babbled. Then he changed, losing verbal and social skills.

Dov was later diagnosed with autism, "a perplexing developmental disorder of the brain that affects his ability to communicate, express emotion and interact with others," writes Craig Tomashoff in a *Family Circle* article.

After a long struggle to understand and cope, Dov's parents, Jonathan Shestack and Portia Iverson, founded CAN (Cure Autism Now) which raises money, supports families and increases public awareness of a disorder said to be more prevalent than cystic fibrosis, Down syndrome or multiple sclerosis.

As one admirer notes, Dov's parents "have taken a personal tragedy and are making life better for children around the world."

Is it possible to bring good out of evil? Some success out of utter failure? It is, if we choose to give life the best that is in us.

As you did it to one of the least of...My family, you did it to Me. (Matthew 25:40)

Holy God, in the face of trials and troubles, may I show courageous persistence.

Christmas Variations

Christmas in New York combines customs from cultures far and wide. While not everyone celebrates Christmas religiously, everyone enjoys the festivities and the spirit of generosity.

Pheur Chantha, a Buddhist from Cambodia, lives in a Bronx apartment with her husband and eight young children. For their benefit, she gets a tree, hangs ornaments, puts up festive lights. "It makes me happy to see all the decorations and the children so happy," she says. "I love Christmas."

Boguslawa Grajdek now celebrates Christmas in Brooklyn. But she comes from Poland where, under Communism, religious expression was as difficult as it was meaningful. On Christmas Eve she and her mother prepare a special pre-midnight Mass supper of 12 meatless dishes. She says, "I like the way they do it here. It's more inclusive."

Every culture and religion has much to teach. We can all benefit by being receptive to new ideas.

Celebrate your festivals. (Nahum 1:15)

May everyone share in the joys of the season, Jesus.

O Christmas Tree

A $5 tip that was refused brought a little Christmas joy into the life of columnist Rick Shefchik.

He and his family purchased their Christmas tree at a nursery. A teenager hauled the tree out to their car. Then, taking off his gloves, he wrapped the tree in twine and scooted under the snow-covered car to secure it to the bumper.

"There's little holiday charm in doing these tasks in sub-zero weather," Shefchik noted. He offered the boy a $5 tip. The young man refused it, saying it was merely his job.

Driving away from the lot, Shefchik reflected that "I met a nice kid who worked hard on a cold day and didn't want anything extra for it," he said. "I hope he has a wonderful Christmas."

Generosity usually means giving, but it could mean not accepting a gift. Whatever you do, be open-hearted in all things.

The measure you give will be the measure you get, and still more will be given you. (Mark 4:24)

Help us remember, Lord, that generosity leads to generosity.

On Wings of Hope

Sometimes it only takes one story to give the world wings. That's what happened in 1962 when a priest, giving a sermon in St. Louis, Missouri, spoke about a nun in Kenya. He told how Sister Teresa Michael, a nurse, flew a plane that was nearly falling apart.

Four men, Bill Edwards, Joe Fabish, George Haddaway, and Paul Rodgers, all had aviation backgrounds and decided to buy and refurbish a Cessna Skywagon for Sister Michael.

Soon the four were flooded with requests for aviation-related assistance. They founded Wings of Hope International.

Today it is the oldest nonsectarian aviation charity in the world and has refurbished and distributed 125 airplanes to organizations in 31 countries.

What need inspires you to charitable deeds today? There is someone you can help, someone to whom you can give hope.

Do not neglect to do good and to share what you have, for such sacrifices are pleasing to God. (Hebrews 13:16)

Strengthen and inspire missionaries and aid workers, Lord.

Home for Christmas

This is the story of a respected man who rose to the pinnacle of success. Upon retiring, he returned to his small hometown in the South.

There, he met a man named Curtis who had grown up in the same town. They enjoyed sharing boyhood memories. When Curtis' wife became ill, the former executive and his wife visited Curtis at home. They were appalled by its ramshackle condition.

Enlisting the help of members of their church and Habitat for Humanity, Jimmy and Rosalyn Carter worked to build Curtis and his wife a decent home. Target date: Christmas.

"We spent the last two days and nights laying carpets and tile floors, planting shrubbery, trimming doors and windows, and hanging paintings on the walls," the former President recounts in his book, "Christmas in Plains." "It was the best Christmas of all."

Giving generously of our time and ourselves to those in need can't help but mean a joyful Christmas.

Stretch out your hand to the poor, so that your blessing may be complete. (Sirach 7:32)

Thank You, God, for those who inspire us to liberality and simplicity.

Sing to the Prince of Peace

The first North American Christmas carol was written for Native Americans living near the St. Lawrence River. It is called The Huron Carol.

Jesous Ahatonia, tells of Jesus' birth in the native language and idiom. It was adapted from a sixteenth-century French folk song by John de Brébeuf, a Jesuit missionary to the Hurons from 1626 until he was martyred in 1649.

The carol is an example of how faith can bridge the chasm between different peoples with creativity and a sensitivity for cultural differences. The Baby Jesus may be wrapped in a robe of "rabbit skin," the shepherds replaced by "hunters," and the gifts of frankincense and myrrh changed into "fox and beaver pelt," but the message is still one of "beauty, peace and joy."

Just as Jesus was born for us, He wants His love to be born in our hearts and shared with one another.

A child has been born for us...and He is named Wonderful Counselor, Mighty God, Everlasting Father, Prince of Peace. (Isaiah 9:6)

Infant Jesus, foster abiding love among all Your children.

A Timeout in War

When Bertie Felstead died at age 106, he was the last-known surviving member of a British battalion that played an impromptu soccer game with their German counterparts on Christmas day, 1915. That truce only lasted a half-hour, but it was a poignant and memorable moment in a time of carnage.

Felstead was in a trench near a snowy French village, listening as German soldiers sang Christmas carols. The British responded in kind. And early on Christmas day, "a few of the Germans...walked over to us. A whole mass of us went out to meet them. Nothing was planned." The soldiers smoked shared cigarettes and "chatted," as an informal soccer match began. "There could have been 50 on each side," Felstead remembered. "No one kept score."

Years later, Felstead would say, "There wouldn't have been a war if it had been left to the public."

We all have an obligation to seek justice, mercy and peace.

If you had walked in the way of God, you would be living in peace forever. (Baruch 3:13)

Guide us to peaceful solutions in all our endeavors, Spirit.

Deciding To Be Happy

Hirotada Ototake is the young author of a book that has sold almost 5,000,000 copies in his native Japan alone. The book is entitled *No One's Perfect,* and is the inspiring and upbeat autobiography of a person born without arms or legs.

"Everyone just assumes that the disabled are people you feel sorry for," the now famous writer says. "But I am not pitiful. I enjoy my life, and I want to tell people that." His book is credited with changing the way many people view those with disabilities, and heightened awareness even brought about a law that will improve wheelchair access to public facilities in Japan.

Ototake has confronted challenges in his life most of us can hardly imagine, much less overcome.

Here is some simple wisdom imparted by a young man who writes by holding a pen between his cheek and the stub of his left arm: "You alone decide if you're going to be happy."

You are the light of the world...let your light shine before others, so that they may see your good works and give glory to your Father in heaven. (Matthew 5:14,16)

Lord Jesus, I choose Your way, the way of light.

Raising Heroes

How can you make a hero of your child? Psychologist Ervin Staub offers parents these techniques:

- Start with small, safe steps. Safe ways to practice heroism include showing compassion for a bully's victim or speaking to those in a crowd about how bullying is wrong without confronting the attacker.

- Make them responsible—and prepare them. Giving youngsters responsibility for animals or other children makes them more caring adults. Also, help them develop skills and the strength they need to do heroic things.

- Set an example—and explain it. Children are more likely to copy altruistic behavior if adults explain their actions.

- Don't pay. Youngsters who are rewarded for good behavior are less likely to help later on.

In the long run, parents can find the answer for building heroes out of their children in a four-letter word: love.

Train children in the right way and when old, they will not stray. (Proverbs 22:6)

May I show Your kindness, Master, to all I meet this day.

Staying in Shape On the Road

A fact of contemporary life is that millions of business-people must travel in order to perform their jobs. Is it possible to stay fit, no matter how much you travel? The answer is "yes" as long as you plan your time and have the right attitude. Here are a few ways to stay in shape when away from home:

- Don't forget to pack your sneakers. Go out for a walk or use the hotel's stairwells and hallways. But do stay aware of safety.

- Find an exercise program on TV and follow along.

- Do sit-ups and pushups while you watch TV.

- Power-walk through the airport terminal.

- Practice yoga poses or other stretches in your room.

While not always easy, it's important to keep fit and healthy. We honor God's gift of life when we do so.

God formed man from the dust of the ground, and breathed into his nostrils the breath of life; and the man became a living being. (Genesis 1:7)

Trinity, inspire me to keep Your gift of my body healthy.

Carving out a Life

Vincent Palumbo, master carver at Washington's National Cathedral, died at 66 after a long battle with leukemia.

His work lives on. "We thank you for reminding us about the great ministry of artists," Dean Nathan Baxter said at Palumbo's funeral. "We thank you for the sermons in stone, wood, iron, and glass, preached to the witness of eternity."

Palumbo, who began carving under the tutelage of his father and grandfather, had a whimsical side. Hidden on the cathedral's exterior is a small statue of his own likeness, hanging from scaffolding.

Palumbo saw his work as a spiritual calling: "The sculptor creates it, but we give it life," he once told the Washington Post. "The original design is like the creation, the plaster model is the death. When we carve it into stone, it is the resurrection."

Life, death, resurrection—a pertinent reminder for us.

A work is praised for the skill of the artisan. (Sirach 9:17)

Let us celebrate Your presence in beauty, Creator God.

The Power of Self

Ralph Waldo Emerson, in his essay, "Self-Reliance," pays homage to the unique abilities that lie within each person. He maintains that to reach our true potential we must first learn to be confident in our abilities.

He writes, "The power that resides in (each person) is new in nature, and none but he knows what that is which he can do, nor does he know until he has tried."

Emerson encourages us to try because he knew that the first obstacle is often our own lack of confidence. But he also realized that others may discourage us from taking action.

How many times have we heard, "It can't be done that way," or "You can't fight city hall?" But does anyone really know that you can't do it, or that you can't fight city hall? Emerson writes, "all history (is)...the biography of a few stout and earnest persons" who believed they could make a difference.

Believing that our individual abilities can change the world is the first step towards actually changing it.

**Act with justice and righteousness.
(Jeremiah 22:3)**

Mighty Lord of Ages, remind me that You give me all I need to do Your will.

Also Available

Have you enjoyed volume 37 of *Three Minutes a Day*? These other Christopher offerings may interest you:

- **News Notes** – published ten times a year on a variety of topics of current interest. One copy as published is free; bulk and standing orders may be arranged.

- **Ecos Cristóforos** – Spanish translations of selected News Notes. Issued six times a year. One copy as published is free; bulk and standing orders may be placed.

- **Wall or Desk Appointment Calendar and Monthly Planner** – The calendar offers an inspirational message for each day as well as for each month. The Monthly Planner with its trim, practical design also offers a monthly inspirational message.

- **Videocassettes** – Christopher videocassettes range from wholesome entertainment to serious discussions of family life and current social and spiritual issues.

For more information on The Christophers or to receive **News Notes, Ecos Cristóforos** or our newest catalog, write:

The Christophers,
12 East 48th Street, NY 10017

Phone: 212-759-4050

Web site: www.christophers.org

E-mail: mail@christophers.org